TRAVEL THE WORLD WITHOUT WORRIES

AN INSPIRATIONAL GUIDE TO LONG-TERM BUDGET TRAVEL

Marek Bron

Brontosaurus
Haarlem, The Netherlands
www.indietraveller.co
Travel the World Without Worries / Marek Bron. —2nd ed.

Contents

"Surely, of all the wonders of the world, the horizon is the greatest."

—FREYA STARK

Foreword

THIS BOOK IS ALL ABOUT helping you achieve your great travel ambitions. If you have ever dreamed of going away for longer than just your typical holiday—if you want to travel the world for many weeks, months, or maybe even a year or beyond—then this guide is for you.

Whether you are planning a round-the-world trip, a career break, a gap year, or a backpacking trip, this book will show you how you can travel further and longer for less. It will guide you step-by-step through all the pre-trip planning and preparation, and it will arm you with a wealth of trail-tested tips and techniques that you can use to make your journey more adventurous and fulfilling.

If you have done it before you will already know this, but it's amazing to go deeper on your travels. The difference between short-term and longer-term travel can be hard to explain, though it reminds me a bit of the difference between snorkelling and scuba diving—two activities that I've often enjoyed while travelling in tropical destinations.

A regular holiday is a bit like snorkelling... it's a lot of fun, but it also has certain limits. You might be able to see some wonderful things on the reef down below, but you are always at the surface level, and you are always on the outside looking in. There might be some amazing things just at arm's length (like obvious tourist spots), but you know that the true wonders lie deeper down below. That is, to me, what being a tourist often feels like. You can only ever dip in a little bit, but you can never go all the way. It's often more difficult to go to places that are a little off-the-beaten-track, and it's more challenging to slow down and get to know places more intimately.

Long-term travel is more like scuba diving. It takes more preparation, and it's maybe a little scary at first. But when you do it, you unlock a whole new world. You can dive down and truly immerse yourself in all the places you go. A bigger trip lets you go deeper, stay longer, and see things that people at the surface will never see.

If you are planning a shorter trip, that's okay; you will still get a ton of valuable travel advice from this book. But if you want to travel for many weeks, many months, or even longer, then the advice in this book will apply perfectly to your situation.

Although I travelled for well over a decade on shorter trips and weekend breaks, it wasn't until my first-ever backpacking trip that I truly I fell in love with travelling. I have been going on big trips ever since. One of these trips lasted an entire two years, taking me gradually through every country in Southeast Asia, and then from Mexico all the way down to Argentina overland. While much of my travels have been in the developing world (as you will notice from many of the examples and anecdotes to come), I have also travelled extensively all over Europe as well as in the United States, Canada, Australia and Japan. Throughout my travels I've kept a blog called Indie Traveller (www.indietraveller.co) where I regularly share inspiration and advice, and which quickly grew into one of the Top 30 most visited travel blogs.

Travel The World Without Worries is essentially the book I wished I had before my first big trip. While it would be silly to claim that you need a book like this to travel the world and come back in one piece, you're likely to make costly, unnecessary, or embarrassing mistakes if you are not adequately prepared.

I myself had to learn some of the lessons the hard way. I once got stranded with a broken car on a mountain in Guatemala at night. I got robbed in broad daylight in Rio De Janeiro. My debit card got swiped and cloned in Honduras and more than $4000 disappeared from my bank account (which thankfully I could still claim back). I once spent the night in a pay-by-the-hour "Love Hotel" thinking it was just a normal hotel, which was just a little awkward. At an airport in Australia my taxi drove off with my luggage still in the trunk, and when I ran after it with my arms flailing the airport terror alert got triggered causing police to swarm on my position (I got my luggage back eventually). I lost my smartphone in the jungles of Laos, got scammed a dozen times in Vietnam, and got a nasty ear infection in Thailand for which a village doctor inexplicably gave me a jab in my butt (somehow I was concerned that he'd not noticed me frantically pointing at my ears).

Of course, these are just a handful of extreme anecdotes from several years of constant travel. The challenges you normally face will be no more extreme than figuring out which bus to take next, or finding a place to sleep for the night. But even such basic challenges can seem difficult, especially if you haven't had to deal with them in foreign countries before (or maybe just not for many weeks or months on end).

This book incorporates all the lessons I've learned, as well as many insights shared with me by the countless travellers that I've been so fortunate to meet on my journeys. By the end of this book, you will be able to hit the ground running and travel with confidence. While you will no doubt still feel giddy when you get off that plane and set forth into the unknown, you can feel assured that you have thought of everything.

The chapters in this book are mostly self-contained so that you can jump around to find specific answers if you'd like, though it is best to read the book sequentially. It roughly follows a chronological order, starting with pre-trip planning, onto life on the trail, and finally coming back home.

Good luck, and bon voyage!

Dear International Reader

This book makes no assumptions about where you are from. I myself am Dutch, speak English with an American accent, but live in the UK. I typically use US Dollars when I travel, but use British Pounds or Euros at home. This book features a mish-mash of currencies, its spelling is British, but some of the measurements are metric. I know, it's a mess, though this is what happens when you become a world nomad!

I have tried to include conversions where possible, though truly this book is intended for anyone from any country. If nothing else, it might help you get accustomed to dealing with such international differences, as you will no doubt have to on your travels... (By the way, if you ever need to convert units or currencies, you can simply use Google. For example, try typing "100 dollars in euro", and you will get the answer straight away.)

[1]

The world is your oyster

CHANCES ARE THAT YOU CAN travel further and longer than you think.

When I talk about my travels with people who have never spent more than a week or two at a time abroad, I always hear the same things: "well, *you* could do that, but my situation is different", or "I would travel too if only I had the money."

More often than not, these are people who could easily go on a big journey if that's what they truly wanted.

All too often, limiting beliefs hold us back from being as ambitious with our travel plans as we would really like to be. The truth is that you can achieve great things even on a modest budget, and that you can travel far and wide despite the obstacles seemingly in your way.

If you are reading this book, then you surely are already dreaming about exploring the world. But before we get into the nitty-gritty of how to plan, prepare, and pack for a trip, perhaps we should first examine those limiting beliefs. After all, who knows? Maybe you are still setting your sights a little too low...

Iguazu Falls, Brazil

Finding the time to travel

If you are a student or graduate, count yourself lucky because you are in a life phase with fewer commitments than most. For you, money is probably the main limiter rather than time, so simply try to travel for as long as you can or want to. Go with the wind, young grasshopper!

If you have bigger life commitments, then these might seem like difficult obstacles in the way of travelling for a long time.

Your job is likely to be the main obstacle. In some cultures it is not too uncommon to take extended time off (for instance, in many countries in Europe). In the US, this can be almost unheard of. However, trying to get a leave of absence is always worth a shot.

Some long-term travellers make agreements with their employer allowing them to take unpaid time off and return to their jobs after their trip. This is not just possible within, say, cushy internet start-ups eager to please their star employees; for example, I met a psychotherapist who got three months of unpaid leave, and a call centre worker who was able to get away for six weeks. Usually such arrangements take advantage of a slow period within the organisation. It's a win-win, as the employer can reduce their overhead for a while, and will get you back later fully refreshed and already trained on the job.

If you are trying to get away for a not-too-crazy amount of time, for instance a month, this can potentially be done through a combination of paid and unpaid leave. While on a permanent contract I once managed to double my time off by requesting additional unpaid leave on top of my accrued holiday. I made the argument that I had a unique travel opportunity (but that I didn't want to quit my job over), and that I had gone beyond the call of duty at work in recent months. It's somewhat gutsy and you clearly have to be tactful in discussing such options, but you will never know without trying.

Some people manage to actually take their job with them on the road. Increasingly it's possible for knowledge workers to continue working while they are abroad, so long as they have a laptop and an internet connection. We get into this topic a lot more in *Chapter 3: Financing your travels*.

In some work cultures it's entirely acceptable for someone to take a one-time career sabbatical, though you have to be lucky to live in a country where this is expected and supported (hello, Sweden!).

The ultimate way to travel long-term, however, is to not have a job at all. This might sound extreme, but it's the only way to be truly free. Many world travellers either ditch their jobs, or were laid off and found in this the impetus to travel.

Admittedly it can be difficult to even imagine quitting your job to travel, and doing so might not be right for everyone. That said, often the fears associated with quitting have little to do with the realities. If you managed to get your current job, chances are you can find another one like it in the future. Keep in mind that in an increasingly globalised world, having some international experience can be a real asset. Travel can look great on a C.V., so long as you frame it as a valuable experience. Don't just make it sound like you were sipping mojitos on a beach the whole time; focus on the valuable aspects of travel such as budgeting, negotiation, or soft skills like self-reliance and communication.

While only you can make an informed decision about whether to quit your job, do make sure that you consider the risk of future regret and weigh this against any perceived risks to your career now. Will an entirely safe career path still make you happy many years from now, or will you be wondering why you never went on that big travel adventure when you had the chance?

The problem is that it's all too easy to become over-invested in your career, always hanging on for the next promotion or that next pay-check. With career blinders on, things that ultimately don't matter so much seem to matter the world to you then (such as that next project, your next employee evaluation, or next year's financial targets). I constantly meet travellers around the world who are thankful to have stepped out of that treadmill, at least for a little while.

Think of travel as a regret avoidance strategy. I know quite a few people who have regrets about not having travelled when they had the opportunity, but I have not spoken to a single person who travelled and had any woes about it afterwards. Imagine what you'll be telling your grandchildren about one day: will it be that time you were still working in that soul-destroying job... or the time you were on a grand adventure filled with magic and wonder? (Hint: one of these does not make for great story time material...)

Dealing with life commitments

Besides a job, there might be other commitments keeping you from travelling longer.

If you own a house or if you're on a tenancy contract, this can almost feel like this is physically tying you down. Wouldn't it be great if you could tie 20,000 balloons to the roof of your house and fly away like Carl Fredricksen in the movie *Up*? Sadly, this is not very practical. A better solution is to sublet your place, or to move out and temporarily put your belongings into storage. The pros and cons of doing so are covered further in *Chapter 3: Financing your travels*.

Santorini Island, Greece

You would think that in certain situations you would be absolutely mad to go on a big trip. I once thought that once you have a family with kids you'll definitely have to put any grand travel ambitions on ice until the kids are grown up... but then I met a whole bunch of travelling families and my perspective of what's possible changed completely.

For instance, I met a family with three children travelling for a whole year. In Panama I met a family who sold their car, bought a boat, and went sailing around the world (their plan was to sell the boat again when they get back home). I even met a couple who were backpacking through Vietnam for two months with an infant. I imagine this must not be particularly easy, but it just goes to show you that people out there are doing things that many people would not think possible.

Of course, maybe you don't have a family or any dependants. The broader point here is that if people with huge life responsibilities can travel the world, then surely so can you. Whatever is keeping you fixed in one place, there are always creative solutions that still let you travel.

It ain't easy being American

While the world is truly your oyster, prying open that oyster can admittedly be more difficult for Americans.

If you live in the United States, you will likely face more impediments to long-term travel than most people from other Western countries. Being European myself, it took quite a few conversations with Americans for me to realize just how different things are in the US.

The first impediment is time. The US has no required vacation time, and what little vacation time you do get you often can't just use up all at once. Many employees also fear that if they leave their post for longer than a week they will be seen as non-essential to the business. There is relatively little support in the US for, say, going a 4 or 6-week summer trip, let alone a gap year or career break. (Contrast this to countries like the UK or Australia, where going on at least one big trip is seen by many as almost a rite of passage.) This means that international travel is often not the norm in the US, and when Americans do get a rare chance to travel, they're more likely to do so domestically and for a shorter period of time.

The other impediment is money. For instance, while college tuition is heavily subsidized or even completely free in other countries (hooray for socialist democracies!), Americans often find themselves knee-deep in debt upon graduating. That's not exactly a great starting point from which to then go gallivanting around the globe without a care in the world. And once you're part of the working world, you might find that work responsibilities never stop.

Add to that a US news media that makes it seem as though the world is a hundred times more dangerous than it actually is, and you can see why round-the-world and overseas backpacking trips just don't have quite as much cultural acceptance.

So what's the answer? It's probably that, as an American, you have to be a little foolhardier than others to realize your travel dreams. It's no coincidence that US travel blogs present longer-term travel as a radical lifestyle choice, sometimes with a hint of "f--- the system" attitude. You might have to work harder to get past the bigger you face, and friends and family might not always fully understand what you're trying to do. More practically speaking, you can try to integrate your travels into your career path at least to some degree, for instance by including work or volunteering experience into your trip, or you could even take your work with you on the road. This topic is covered in more detail in *Chapter 3. Financing your travels.*

Trip financing: where there's a will...

You don't need to be rich to travel the world. You will, however, need a willingness to save up and to travel in smart ways.

If your funds are limited, your best bet is to go to countries that are cheap. It's no accident that this book focuses a lot on Asia and Latin America, as travelling in many countries there is inexpensive (especially for anyone on a Western income), making them ideally suited to long-term travel.

Costs vary per country, but there are many places around the world where you can travel comfortably for around $1000 a month, sometimes even less. By avoiding expensive destinations in more developed economies, you can increase the length of your trip dramatically.

The other option is to travel to more expensive countries, but to use all sorts of cost-saving strategies and travel hacks to still make this sustainable in the longer term.

A trip lasting a couple of months might require at least a couple of grand. This is not nothing, but it's within range of most people who can set aside a little money for their travel fund every month. Maybe not everyone will be able to finance a big trip as quickly or as easily, but where there's a will there's always a way.

I'm often asked how much it costs to travel for a whole year (as travelling for roughly one year is a common goal for a big round-the-world trip). However, asking "how much is a year of travel?" is kind of akin to asking "how big is a fish?". It all depends... are we talking about a dwarf goby, or a whale shark? A year-long journey can be as cheap or as expensive as you make it. Though if you target budget destinations only, you could travel for a whole year starting at about $10,000. (And there are some exceptionally thrifty people who do it for even less.) Again, this is not nothing, but it's far from the millionaire status that some people think you need in order to go on a very big journey.

In *Chapter 2: Getting inspired*, we'll discuss the financial pros and cons of travelling in different parts of the world, and we'll look at some popular trips of varying lengths (from about a month up to a year or more). In *Chapter 3*, we'll cover how you can determine your budget, use a plethora of methods to save up money, and how you can use all manner of creative ways to finance your trip.

Atacama Desert, Chile

Is long-term travel a wise investment?

Wait a minute—is it a good idea to spend a lot of money on what are ultimately just fleeting one-off experiences? Isn't it better to invest in more tangible or material things that will continue to benefit you for many years? It only seems logical that buying a physical object that lasts longer will pay off much more.

Numerous psychologists have actually studied this issue and have come to one conclusion: while buying things doesn't make you unhappy, it doesn't make you happy. There is a brief period of satisfaction after buying a new thing, but you adapt to this new thing very quickly, after which it becomes normal to you.

Experiences, on the other hand, become a bigger part of ourselves than any material objects ever can. They give us lasting memories, which can never be taken away from us. Experiences also become part of our identities, and we can share and talk about them with others for the rest of our lives.

While it's true that much of the enjoyment of your trip takes place during your trip, you'll still be enjoying the afterglow for many years to come. So, to answer the question, travel is definitely worth the investment!

Why you should travel independently

Going on an organized tour is easy and convenient, but it's not the same as doing things on your own.

When it's just you on the open road to destiny, your journey truly becomes your own. You can go to places that tours never go to, tailor your trip exactly to your interests, and stay longer or shorter in places depending on how you feel.

If you haven't travelled independently before (or just not on a big journey), it might seem a little daunting to have to do everything on your own. Independent travel is admittedly not without its challenges, but that's also what makes it ultimately so rewarding. Even the little setbacks along the way can later turn into good stories.

If you are wondering how to go about making your day-to-day decisions, how to book things, plan things, get tickets for buses or trains, and all the other practical on-the-ground aspects of travel, all such issues are covered in *Chapter 4. Finding your way.*

Besides giving you the freedom to do whatever you want, travelling independently also lets you make dramatic savings over any packaged tour or holiday. The prices advertised by the travel industry are not the kind of prices you should expect when travelling entirely according to your own plans.

To illustrate, I just looked up a 30-day tour through Peru, Argentina and Brazil with a budget oriented group tour operator. The price? A dizzying €5160 per person, excluding flights (that's about $6000 or £3600). For that kind of money, you could easily spend half a year backpacking through South America (in other words *six times longer!*). Suddenly this tour operator does not seem so 'low budget' anymore. While pre-packaged tours are nice if you want to have everything arranged for you, they come with a considerable price tag.

Overcoming your fears

It is easy, and in a way even logical, to fear the unknown. If you have never been to a particular country or continent before, you will have almost no frame of reference. It's no surprise that a lot of the e-mail I get from readers of my blog have an air of nervous excitement. Many of the questions I get essentially boil down to "I really want to do this, but I'm also a little scared... what should I do?".

To go on a great journey you will have to get past those initial fears, or at least be willing to take a leap of faith. What can help you in getting more comfortable is to research and absorb a lot of information, as this can turn your travel goals from an abstract and distant idea into something much more tangible that you know you can actually do (reading this book will certainly help with this!).

Besides the purely practical aspects of travel, you might also wonder about safety. Fortunately, the reality is that most countries are perfectly safe to visit. Even in countries that do have some safety issues, the concerns are usually limited to a few specific and easily avoidable areas. Many tips and tricks on how to stay safe and travel responsibly can be found in *Chapter 8: Personal safety and security*.

Another common fear is the fear of travelling solo. Since it can be difficult to find a travel buddy for a longer trip, many people will set out on their own. But this can raise all sorts of questions about whether you're going to meet any people or whether things will be lonely. If these are issues you're facing, the last couple of chapters in this book can really help you along, as they are dedicated to all the social aspects of travel as well as offering specific advice for travelling solo.

While deciding to travel can be a little scary, once you are on your trip you will surely find that travelling itself is not scary at all. Going on a journey can be a fantastic life-affirming experience, and with the right knowledge and preparation you can ensure you'll have a successful trip.

Island hopping, Bacuit Archipelago in the Philippines

You can go anywhere... but it's not always easy

While independent travel is unquestionably wonderful, it should be said that it can also be hard work at times. Sometimes you are stuck on an uncomfortable creaky bus for hours on end, spending ages just figuring out how to book a ticket, or cursing to yourself while hauling a heavy backpack around town. This is all part of the adventure, though it can also wear you down.

Of course, travelling is not hard work in the same way that working in a coal mine trying to make an honest living is hard work. But it does take a bit more effort than a regular holiday. If you want to *only* relax all the time, you might not like life on the road. Sometimes you have to deal with long transit times, delays, and other frustrating challenges before you can ultimately reap your rewards.

That said, the hardships of backpacking are also often exaggerated. Many travellers emphasize only the extremes as it makes for better stories. Will you tell people about the days you just spent lazying in your hammock, or the time your bus broke down and you had to plough through a thunderstorm with 15 kg on your back? Clearly, the stories that get shared the most are all the cool "war stories", not the times that people had it easy.

Travel blogs and other media further reinforce the image of world travel being necessarily very hardcore. A good example is the movie *The Beach*, which is often a prime source of inspiration for those wanting to go to Southeast Asia. In this movie, Leonardo DiCaprio's character finds himself in a hostel in Bangkok that frankly looks terrifying, with dirty mattresses, graffiti-covered concrete walls and no windows anywhere. It seems even a North Korean prison cell would offer a more uplifting atmosphere than what is depicted in this film. While rooms like this do surely exist in some places, you will generally find clean, comfortable, and homely accommodation in a country like Thailand, sometimes for as little as five dollars a night.

In other words, while world travel won't constantly bathe you in luxury, you also won't have to travel like you are Bear Grylls on a survival mission, subsisting solely on a diet of dung beetles. Just make sure you are the kind of pragmatic person who would enjoy travelling on a budget.

If that sounds good to you, then try to carve out as much time for your journey as you possibly can. Find creative solutions to anything that might stand in the way of your travel ambitions, because once you're on the trail you will surely wish you could travel longer.

Ultimately, how long you could or should go away depends on numerous factors, all of which are very personal. But no matter your circumstances, consider all your options and find out how long you want your trip to truly be. For some, the answer may simply be to travel as long as they can before their money runs out. For others, there will be a specific beginning and end date.

Once you know how long you want to go away, you can start thinking about where exactly you want to go. Conveniently, this is covered in the next chapter...

[2]

Getting inspired

DECIDING WHERE TO GO can be difficult. The world is such a big place that you can easily become paralysed by choice.

Before I went on my first big journey, all I knew was that I wanted to get away for a while. I had no idea where to go. I taped a world map to my wall, blindfolded myself, and threw a dart at the map. Fate would show me the way! Then I hit Somalia... shit.

While I was looking for adventure, spending time in a failed state torn apart by warring factions was not exactly high on my bucket list. So I told myself this initial dart throw was just a practice round and that the next one would be for real. I threw again and hit the very north tip of Greenland, an area with nothing but ice and rocks for thousands of miles.

So the dart board technique pretty much sucks.

If you want to travel abroad, it's best to carefully research your options and then to make a reasoned decision for where to go. There are certainly some romantic tales out there of people catching a last-minute flight to some entirely unplanned destination, but this approach is more suited to international fugitives than to travellers looking for specific experiences. Not knowing anything about where you're going will surely lead to disappointment, or worse.

The challenge is to go somewhere that not only suits your goals and interests, but also matches your level of travel experience. Where you go enormously affects your budget requirements as well, and in turn your whole approach to your journey. For example, it can take a lot of dedication and creativity to make travel sustainable in the long term when focusing only on expensive Western countries. Go to inexpensive developing countries and the financial aspects of your trip will be much easier to manage, rewarding you with a greater sense of freedom as well.

While there are many things to take into account, the inspiration phase can be a lot of fun. Researching different countries and regions, imagining all those far-flung wonders of the world, and letting yourself get excited about it all is a big part of your journey—that is, before it has even started yet.

This chapter aims to give you a high-level overview of some of the options that are out there: different ways to travel the world, different high-level routes to consider, and different sources of inspiration for you to dig into. More specific trip planning is covered in *Chapter 4: Finding your way*, which deals with such topics as itinerary planning, accommodation booking, and managing the day-to-day decisions of your journey. For now, let's simply dream of the broader possibilities.

What is the purpose of your trip?

A big trip doesn't necessarily need a purpose: its purpose can simply be for you to have fun. But thinking about a purpose can help give it some focus. Do you wish see all the places you always dreamed of seeing? Is your goal to become a wiser and more travelled person? Do you want to volunteer abroad? Maybe you are interested in a very active journey, or maybe you are simply drawn by the siren call of that hammock and mojito on a secluded beach.

I have met many couples whose goal it was to see the world as far and wide as possible before buying a house and settling down. The goal, then, becomes to see as much of the world as possible while this is relatively easier. For many, travelling includes an element of self-development. For instance, many younger travellers hit the trail not just to see the world but to discover a greater sense of independence within themselves.

Travel goals can be as specific or as broadly defined as you want. For instance, I recently spent time with travellers whose aim it was to surf all the famous surf breaks of the world, while getting to know each country along the way. Arbitrary milestones can also make for a good trip: a journey from the northern most tip to the southernmost tip of Europe will certainly lead you to unexpected adventures.

Give some thought as to why you are excited about going on a journey. Your answers to this question can help you steer towards specific regions or countries around the world. It can even inform your travel style. Those wishing to have a deeply shared experience with their travel companions may wish to plan a road trip far into territory unknown, where it's truly just you versus the world. Or perhaps you would plan a hiking adventure in the Himalayas where you'll be heavily reliant on each other. The solo adventurer may wish to challenge themselves to get out of their comfort zone and join up with other solo travellers in popular backpacker destinations—where hostels buzz with activity and ad hoc travel plans emerge among strangers at breakfast tables every morning.

Keep in mind that, as cliché as it sounds, it is ultimately the journey and not just the destination that counts. What you often end up remembering most fondly are not the much-expected highlights you planned in advance, but the little unexpected moments along the way. Visiting the ancient Inca ruins of Machu Picchu could be a glorious experience, or it could be a bit of a let-down depending on your circumstances, expectations, or the weather. But spend enough time in South America and you can be assured you'll come back with plenty of unique stories of your own, ones that couldn't have come from any travel guide or bucket list, but which can easily rival the world wonders or famous attractions you may be dreaming of now.

Travel is meant to be unpredictable. Sometimes the most difficult journeys can be the most rewarding, or the most serendipitous situations the most memorable. Thinking about the goals or purpose of your journey now is like building a kind of scaffolding; something that can give it some initial form and shape.

Sources of travel inspiration

When fishing for travel ideas, why not cast a wide net? Travel blogs and wikis can give much initial inspiration, though there are many other ways to get excited about different parts of the world.

Guidebooks are the more traditional way of finding information. Fortunately, you don't need to buy every guidebook out there just to get some general ideas for where to go. For instance, on the Lonely Planet website (www.lonelyplanet.com) you can download PDFs of the overview maps and introduction chapter of every guide for free. The website of Rough Guides (www.roughguides.com) provides excellent high-level overviews, along with helpful lists of 'Things Not To Miss'. I often like to look in second-hand book stores for cheap used guidebooks—their specific restaurant and accommodation recommendations may be out of date, but the more general info usually still holds up. For a couple of bucks, you will get a wealth of ideas.

Coffee table books can make your daydreaming phase more fun as well. Lonely Planet has two books called *1000 Ultimate Experiences* and *1000 Ultimate Sights*, both containing amazing photography and bite-sized information. Other highly visual and browsable books include *500 of the World's Greatest Trips* by National Geographic and *1000 Places To See Before You Die*. A personal favourite of mine is *Off the Tourist Trail: 1000 Unexpected Travel Alternatives* by Eyewitness Travel. (Hmm, what *is* it with the number 1000?). This book leads you to lesser-known alternatives to all the famous (but often way overcrowded) sights, festivals, natural wonders and beaches around the world—helping you go beyond the standard itinerary items.

Social media is another great place to look. Pinterest is overflowing with travel inspiration boards, which you can easily find through a basic search. On Facebook, one of the best travel inspiration pages is at www.facebook.com/placestosee. On Twitter, take a look at @TheBucktList or @BestEarthPix. Do keep in mind that the superb photos posted here—often heavily colour-corrected or taken from sweeping aerial viewpoints—do make some places look much more majestic than they are in reality. Still, browsing these fantastic photos can trigger all kinds of further research.

The website Atlas Obscura (www.atlasobscura.com) is a growing collaborative encyclopaedia of remarkable and quirky places around the world. Here you'll find such gems as a crater in Turkmenistan that permanently spews fire following a drilling accident in the 1970s, or a church in Portugal that's entirely constructed out of human bones.

Finally, there are some excellent TV shows and documentaries that can give you a real taste of what it's like to travel the world. Some of the best ones are highlighted a little further into this chapter.

The case for developing countries

While you should let your personal travel goals and desires lead you to whatever places fascinate you most, if you find yourself considering only the most expensive countries, you may wish to broaden your horizons.

It can be tempting to focus your research purely on the more familiar and more mainstream destinations in the Western world. Unfortunately, these countries also tend to be quite expensive to travel in, making them less ideal for long-term travel.

A week in, say, Paris can be quite manageable if that's what your entire holiday consists of, but if you're travelling for months on end then such a place can be unreasonably pricey (unless you are particularly crafty at keeping your expenses down—but even then it won't be so easy). When planning a world trip, try going outside your comfort zone and consider some less developed places that may offer better bang for your buck—especially in the long run.

Given the varying levels of economic development around the world, the reality is that for the same cost of travelling two months in Europe you could travel at least half a year in South-East Asia. Trips that are very heavily city-focused also cost a lot more than exploring countries at large. Maybe the Big Ben, Tokyo Tower or the Statue of Liberty can wait until later (perhaps you can see them on individual city trips) while you use the opportunity now to go deeper into other parts of the world.

Low-cost countries are truly where long-term travel becomes the most liberating. If you are from a Western or high-income country, you will have a lot of purchasing power there. In places like Nicaragua, Vietnam, Bolivia or Nepal (just to name a few), your day-to-day financial concerns can easily fade into the background, letting you simply focus on what you would like to do next.

Want to eat a nice meal? When it's just $3 you don't really have to think twice about ordering. Want to hire a local private guide to take you out hiking for a day? When it's only $10 this becomes an entirely low-risk decision. Maybe you get unlucky and that hiking trip ends up being not that amazing, but then at least you won't have to beat yourself up about the money you spent. Such low prices make long-term travel not only more broadly attainable, but they can put you in a very different mind-set. You soon start thinking more in terms of sheer possibilities, and less in harsher terms of cost versus outcome.

Trip financing and budgeting are covered in more detail later, but for now let's consider what are essentially the four basic categories of long-term travel (warning, some generalizations to follow!):

1. Travel like a bum in cheap countries

(Annual cost: $6000+, Monthly cost: $500+)

This is the absolute most basic way to travel the world. It requires focusing exclusively on the cheapest countries around the world, as well as being very disciplined in the way you travel. This is the category of the vagabonds and the drifters with only the smallest of shoestring budgets.

Maybe you could spend time in off-the-beaten-track Central America sleeping only in your own tent or hammock, eating cheap buffet meals (and saving leftovers for later), hitch-hiking, and only going on activities that are free. You could go to India and fully immerse yourself in the local lifestyle, avoiding any of the popular tourist sites, and moving from place to place in crowded 3rd class train carriages only.

This is travel for the ultimate free birds, content to spend much of their days plucking their guitar, or earning a little money by making friendship bracelets and selling them to other travellers (I'm somewhat stereotyping the "hippie traveller" here, but you get my point...). It's not necessarily a glamorous way to travel, and the financial constraints often mean not being able to see or do that many things in each location. But for some it's the only long-term travel that is attainable—and for a few, it's simply a way of life.

2. Travel comfortably in cheap countries

(Annual cost: $12000+, Monthly cost: $1000+)

Given a reasonable budget you can travel very comfortably in many developing countries around the world (think Latin America, South and South-East Asia, south-eastern Europe, and many parts of Africa). You may have to stay in somewhat rustic places at times and "live like a local" a bit, but you will generally be able to afford an otherwise very comfortable lifestyle with very few real restrictions.

As a rough rule of thumb, it takes about $1000 a month, give or take, to travel in most developing countries. With such a budget, you will be easily able to afford hostel accommodation or basic hotel rooms, go sightseeing whenever you'd like, have sit-down restaurant meals multiple times a day, and move about using local transportation, tourist shuttle services, or the occasional short-distance flight. This style of travel is most commonly associated with backpacking and career break trips; it's a way to see the world that is both rewarding and financially attainable for many.

The standard of living in developing countries may of course be lower than you are used to at home, i.e. don't necessarily expect to get a Danish craft beer with your phở noodles in Vietnam, or for that ramshackle bus in Ecuador to be exactly on time. However, once you adjust to the local pace and lifestyle, you can feel like you truly have everything you need.

3. Travel like a bum in expensive countries

(Annual cost: $25000+, Monthly cost: $2100+)

Travelling long-term in expensive countries can be astronomically expensive if you travel the same way you would on a regular holiday. The cost of hotels alone can send your budget spiralling out of control. The alternative is to find creative ways to travel cheaply in expensive countries.

This could mean using basic hostels or hospitality exchanges like CouchSurfing for accommodation. You may have to cook your own meals in hostel kitchens, eat lots of instant noodles, packed lunches, or cheaper fast-food meals. You will typically avoid expensive tours and activities, and instead enjoy publicly accessible sights or go on free city walking tours.

You may not have to go to *quite* these extremes if you limit your overall time in expensive countries and budget adequately. It's no coincidence that many travellers opt to go to Europe, Australia, or the U.S. for maybe one or two months—and not ordinarily for, say, half a year or a year, as this is much more difficult to sustain. (When travellers claim they've been travelling in Western countries for a longer time, they will usually have also worked for at least part of that period.)

4. Travel like a big shot in expensive countries

(Annual cost: $100000+, Monthly cost: $8000+)

When money is of virtually no concern, you can truly go everywhere and do anything... though this is clearly well out of range for most people.

One notable travel blogger, who has travelled non-stop for 7 years running, once privately shared that he spends well over $100000 a year. He acquired his fortune by selling his internet business during the late 90ies dotcom boom. With such financial resources available, you can clearly book any long-distance flight without thinking twice, or spend ample time in hotels in expensive places like Dubai, Fiji, French Polynesia, Monaco, and so on. If this were you, clearly you would not be reading this book and you would already be sipping $20 cocktails in a Presidential Suite somewhere...

Looking at the four categories above, this book focuses a lot on category two: travelling long-term, and with reasonable comfort, in countries where the cost of travel is relatively low. This approach provides the greatest sense of freedom, takes you beyond your comfort zone into exotic places, but is also financially attainable for many. This book also regularly touches on category 3: travelling for an extended period of time in more expensive countries, but without burning a hole in your pocket.

The other extremes don't feature as much. So if you are planning to travel like a tramp with just a bag on a stick or, on the flip-side, if you will be jet-setting around the world while ordering bottle service and 'making it rain', then some of the advice that follows might not apply fully to your situation. In the following chapters, we will look mainly at how you can travel the world on an average person's budget.

The main point I wanted to leave you with however is that cheaper countries are simply great for long-term travel. When you are researching destinations, be sure to give them serious consideration. Further along in this chapter, we will look at more specific examples of destinations or regions where you can get by even on a modest budget.

The difference in cost of travel between places can sometimes make your head spin. Recently in England I took a train from Brighton to London, which lasted about an hour and cost 22 pounds (which is about 33 Dollars or 32 Euro). This really raised my eyebrows as it happened to be exactly my average daily spending on a recent trip in Indonesia. In other words, for the price of just one short train journey in England, I could spend an entire day in Indonesia, easily covering all my transportation, accommodation, meals and sightseeing. Such contrasts can really give you pause.

It's possible that you are much more keen on going to developed countries. If so, just keep those cheaper countries in the back of your mind for potential future trips (they'll be making regular appearances throughout this book).

Round-the-world or overland

When brainstorming your journey, another key consideration comes into play: do you want to go deep, or do you want to go wide?

That is to say, are you planning one grand tour around the world—flying from continent to continent—or are you more interested in travelling overland through a specific part of the world? There are essentially two major styles of world travel: one called round-the-world (or RTW) travel and the other called overlanding. Each can give you a dramatically different experience.

Round the World (RTW) trips are usually organised around a special RTW airline ticket that allows you to fly around the globe in one direction (e.g. west-to-east or east-to-west) while making a set number of stops along the way. For example, an RTW trip may start in London, on to Bangkok, Sydney, Fiji, Los Angeles, New York and then back to London. These RTW flights are offered for one combined price, which is often much cheaper than buying each flight separately.

While you will have to lock in all the RTW stops prior to departure, you will have some flexibility on the dates, which you can typically still change during your trip (sometimes for a fee). You will usually have to complete this multi-stop route within a maximum period of one year. Most RTW packages are limited to flights within a certain airline alliance only.

RTW tickets can be a good option if you want to visit multiple continents, though bear in mind you can only go in one direction, and you are limited to flying only to your pre-chosen destinations. There's no room for any sweeping itinerary changes, so you have to plan things ahead with a bit more care.

Travel agencies such as Kilroy, STA Travel and Airtreks specialize in part in providing RTW tickets. You can also check directly with the airline alliances such as Star Alliance, One World, SkyTeam and The Great Escapade (the last one is not an alliance, but an RTW program shared between Air New Zealand, Virgin Atlantic and Singapore Airlines). Searching online for "RTW itineraries" or searching the hashtag #rtwnow on social media can give you further inspiration for this style of travel planning.

Overlanding is in many ways the opposite approach to round-the-world. Here you only fly in to your starting point and then follow an overland route—travelling primarily by bus, train or personal transportation—until you reach the end of your route.

Sometimes your starting and end point will be the same: this is common in South-East Asia for example where many backpackers travel in a circle that brings them back to a major hub like Bangkok or Singapore, where their return flight awaits. Sometimes the starting and end points will be different: this is common in Latin America where one might start north in, say, Mexico City or Bogotá and end south in Buenos Aires or Rio de Janeiro. Many overland travellers do not book their return flight at all until much later, preferring to have an open jaw trip that gives them greater flexibility.

There are some important pros and cons to both RTW and overland travel:

Round-the-world trip

- **Gives you the most variation.** You will visit a series of completely different destinations on several different continents.
- **Typically good value-for-money for flights.** Since you are buying your flights as one big package, the total price is often quite attractive.
- **But can be much more expensive overall.** Most round-the-world routes go via major hub cities in expensive countries. In the earlier example above, Bangkok would be relatively affordable, but you will have to spend heavily during your stays in New York, Los Angeles or Sydney.
- **Requires more backtracking.** With a round-the-world ticket you always need to backtrack to your prior point of arrival in order to fly to your next stop. This can be costly, time-consuming, or just annoying (as you'll have to retread old ground). For example, perhaps you land in Sydney, then you travel north along the Gold Coast, but then you won't be able to conveniently continue your trip from Brisbane or Cairns; you will have to go back south to Sydney again in order to fly off to that next continent.
- **Requires more upfront planning.** You will have to figure out your stops and schedule in advance, which reduces your flexibility. Often there is a small financial penalty for changing your flight dates.
- **You will need to pack for multiple climates.** Packing light becomes a bit more challenging, as you will likely need clothes for both summer and winter conditions.

Overlanding or regional trip

- **Can give you the lowest cost of travel.** Taking buses and trains is cheaper than flying. Also, popular overland backpacking routes such as the Banana Pancake trail in South-East Asia and the Gringo Trail in Latin America run almost exclusively through low-cost countries.
- **Goes deep instead of broad.** You will get to experience many countries within the same region, letting you cut deeper into the culture and see more within each destination. On the flip-side, you will have less variation as you won't be trotting multiple continents.
- **Gives a different perspective.** You will see landscapes transition gradually, and can gain a greater appreciation for distances and how places relate to each other. Psychologically, it can feel more like a 'real journey'.
- **You might need to pack for one climate only.** Packing light is a little easier as you can pack only what you need within your region of choice. For South-East Asia for example, you can survive easily just with a bunch of t-shirts, one long-sleeve and one jumper (as far as your upper body clothing goes). Travelling lighter has all sorts of advantages, as described later in this book.
- **Greater flexibility.** The only things set in stone on an overland backpacking trip are your starting and end point (though even the end point can be left to improvisation). This lets you easily adapt your route depending on your evolving travel goals.

The appeal of a round-the-world trip is essentially "seeing the world in one go". Of course that is never truly possible, but that's what a lot of RTW trips at least try to aim for. One day you may find yourself tanning on a tropical beach, the next you're freezing your face off while hiking a glacier in Iceland. If this is going to be your one and only opportunity to travel, then a round-the-world ticket may be the way to go.

The appeal of backpacking overland is that it lets you travel more slowly and discover your own path. The goal is less to "see the whole world" (as impossible a task as this is) but more to have a deeper experience in some part

of the world. It's also the best option if you will be travelling on
you can limit yourself to cheaper destinations. When overlanding and using
whatever ground transport the locals use, you also increase the possibility of
unexpected experiences and encounters with locals.

RTW trips can be a bit like an eclectic "best hits" music album featuring a
range of artists: they span a greater range, but by their very nature can be
shallower as well. Overlanding is more like listening to an album by a single
band—it cuts deeper and it's more of a journey, but it may also offer somewhat less variety.

The distinction between RTW and overland is not always so clear-cut. For
instance, you could spend a few weeks in India, fly to Thailand for a few
months of overlanding through Southeast Asia, and then fly to New Zealand
and spend your final weeks there. Is that an overland trip or a round-the-
world trip? It's neither, really. Both these travel styles sit on opposite sides of
a sliding scale, which you can adjust depending on your travel goals.

Personally, I am very partial to overlanding, as this has a certain romance
that more pre-planned around-the-world itineraries might lack. You sometimes hear of RTW trips that, say, hit up 30+ countries in 6 months by flying
between each and every waypoint, but such a pace seems far too fast to
properly enjoy each location. If you do take the RTW approach, make sure
you leave enough breathing room in your itinerary.

Closed borders and other obstacles

When overlanding, it's not always possible to avoid flights altogether,
due to closed borders or natural barriers. For example, the Darién Gap between Central and South America is effectively closed off, and can only be
crossed by sailing around it or flying. The Sahara Desert creates natural
barriers all around northern Africa, and is hugely impractical to cross
overland. Sea routes between the Philippines and Indonesia, or between
Indonesia and Australia, are essentially non-existent. You can find a world
map indicating most of the major overland barriers at:

www.indietraveller.co/articles/view/map-of-where-to-go-
backpacking

The great overland journeys

There are certain popular backpacker routes around the world which, if you haven't travelled much before, you might well be oblivious to. Before I became a travel addict, I certainly had no clue they existed. While I was aware of, and intrigued by, individual countries (as these get promoted in all sorts of ways, including by tourism boards and travel agencies), I had no idea that there were specific travel circuits that many independent travellers like to follow, often running through multiple countries.

Despite the oft-cited ideals of 'going off the beaten track', the majority of backpackers do travel on clearly identifiable circuits, tending to follow similar routes as they move through a region. These circuits can be elusive at first, as they are not precisely set in stone, nor are they promoted in any sort of official way. Spread mostly through word-of-mouth, these routes are shaped by numerous factors over time including geography, points of interest, ease of access, and the availability of transit connections.

On my first big journey through South-East Asia, I didn't realize I was following an established route until many weeks in. After sharing my travel plans with another backpacker, their response was, "oh, cool, so you're doing the Banana Pancake trail as well!" Umm, banana *what*? I later typed "Banana Pancake trail" into a search engine and discovered that, unbeknownst to me, I had been following this oddly named route almost exactly.

When overlanding, it is often easy and rewarding to slip into one of these well-worn grooves. Like a river carrying a boat downstream, these popular travel routes can take you along for a wonderful ride.

Of course, not everyone travels to exactly the same places, and many will deviate by making excursions into less-travelled areas and places of particular interest. Still, it's helpful to be aware of these main travel arteries, as they can often form the core of your itinerary.

What follows are some descriptions of travel routes that are widely considered to be the 'classics'. While this book isn't intended to be a destination guide (and so I'll resist going into too much detail), knowing about some of the popular routes can aid you in your research phase.

In the end, where you ultimately go will depend much on where you call home, your finances, your particular interests, and so on. For each of the highlighted routes I have specified a challenge level, which is intended only as a very loose indication of how much preparation and/or determination a region or route might require. How easy or difficult a country or region is depends, of course, largely on your individual circumstances and experience, though some regions can be broadly said to be easier than others.

South-East Asia (Banana Pancake Trail)

Challenge Level: *Easy / Moderate*
Typical Length: *3 to 4 months for the central mainland of Thailand / Laos / Cambodia / Vietnam, or up to 6-12 months when including the wider region*

Major cities and points of interest across wider Southeast Asia

South-East Asia is widely considered one of the, if not the, best backpacking regions in the world. It owes this distinction to its low cost of travel, relatively high levels of safety, a wealth of amazing points of interest, and a great network of local transportation links.

South-East Asia is a superb choice for a first backpacking trip (though more experienced world travellers can enjoy this region equally). Many first-timers end up starting in Thailand, where tourism is the most developed, though other countries in the region arguably offer more authentic experiences as Thailand increasingly orients itself towards mass tourism.

The Banana Pancake Trail got its tongue-in-cheek name during the early days of backpacking in Asia. Food vendors and guesthouses began catering to travellers by selling banana pancakes and other comfort foods, giving them some welcome relief from an otherwise rice-only diet. Back then, the availability of banana pancakes would be a sure sign that other foreigners had come before.

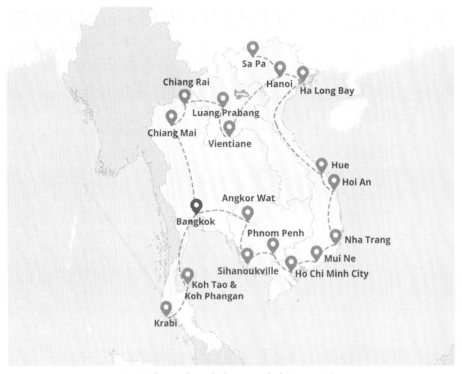

A typical route through the core Indochina countries.

The trail includes places in Thailand (Khao San Road in Bangkok, Pai, the islands of Ko Phangan and Ko Phi Phi), Laos (Luang Prabang and Vang Vieng), Cambodia (Siem Reap and Sihanoukville) and Vietnam (Hanoi, Halong Bay and Hoi An). It has expanded to include parts of Malaysia and Indonesia, with the Gili Islands often a final stop on many South-East Asia tours. The Philippines (El Nido and Borocay Island), India (especially Goa), and parts of southern China are also increasingly seen as part of the Banana Pancake trail, though they are further removed from the main trail running through Indochina.

South-East Asia is well-trodden with constantly growing routes, and it has become somewhat of a backpacker rite of passage. The core countries of Thailand, Laos, Cambodia and Vietnam are the most popular, though a superb network of low-budget airlines, led by carrier AirAsia, makes every other country in the region easily reachable as well. You can travel comfortably for $1000 a month or under, making it ideal for long-term travel.

While there is a slight learning curve and there can be some initial culture shock, most aspects of travelling in this region are rather manageable. Once you have adjusted to travelling in South-East Asia, you will probably find it quite easy—even if you have limited prior travel experience. Language difficulties are negligible, as most people who you will deal with directly (e.g. restaurant staff, receptionists, and so on) will be able to speak at least some basic English. In Malaysia, Myanmar and the Philippines, English is also widely spoken as a second language.

More on South-East Asia:
www.indietraveller.co/articles/view/south-east-asia-itineraries

Central America (Gringo Trail)

Challenge Level: *Moderate*

Typical Length: *2 to 4 months*

Central America encompasses seven small, mostly tropical countries—eight if you count Mexico, which while technically part of North America is often grouped with Central America from a traveller's point of view, as it shares so much culturally with its southern neighbours.

The backpacker route here is known as the Gringo Trail, named after the local slang word for foreigner. This route actually encompasses all of Latin America and roughly follows the Pan-American Highway stretching from Mexico all the way down to Chile. We'll discuss the Central American and South American segments here separately, though going the whole way is also possible (this takes at least about 9 months).

The Central American Gringo Trail starts in Mexico City, then snakes its way down through the Oaxaca and Yucatan regions of Mexico, then down through Belize, Guatemala, Honduras, El Salvador, Nicaragua, Costa Rica and finally Panama. All along this route you will find the usual hostels and tourist infrastructure catering to backpacker travellers. Since the region is quite compact, travel distances in Central America are quite manageable, and transportation is always easy to arrange.

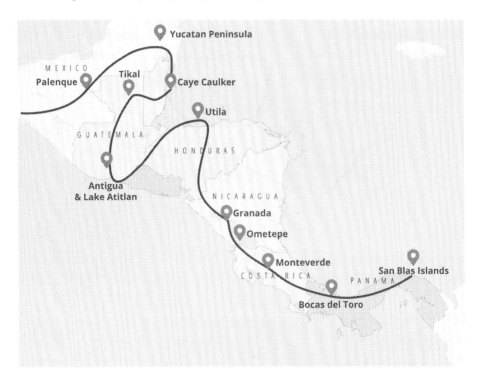

The region is home to much geographic diversity, not to mention impressive remnants of the indigenous Mayan, Aztec and Olmec civilizations, as well as Spanish colonial influences in many of the towns and cities. There are more jungles, lakes, volcanoes and tropical beaches in Central America than you can shake a stick at.

Central America is an amazing part of the world to visit, though it does come with a few challenges. While it is very easy to travel in many parts—especially in Mexico and Costa Rica which both have more developed tourist industries—other parts require at least some level of travel savvy. Honduras and El Salvador in particular suffer from security issues which, while unlikely to be immediately threatening to a visitor, do require some care and due diligence to navigate responsibly.

Another challenge in Central America can be the language, as English is rarely spoken (except for Belize where it is the main language, albeit with a heavy creole accent). If you don't already know some Spanish, taking some lessons can be hugely valuable. That said, if your interactions are limited to people working in hostels/hotels or as tourist guides, you can still make due in Central America without knowing Spanish—you might just be missing out on a lot of the local flavour.

The cost of travel in Central America is quite variable. Most countries are very inexpensive, though Belize and Costa Rica are major exceptions where prices are at near-Western levels at times and where you will need to budget appropriately.

On average, travellers here tend to be a little older and more experienced than the ones who visit Europe or Australia. While Southeast Asia is arguably a better region for first-time backpackers thanks to its high levels of safety and easy travel connections, Central America can equally be tackled as a first trip so long as you are aware of the safety advice and don't mind the slightly higher language barriers (if you don't speak Spanish, that is).

More on Central America:
www.indietraveller.co/articles/view/backpacking-in-central-america

South America (Gringo Trail)

Challenge Level: *Moderate*

Typical Length: *4 to 8 months*

The South American Gringo Trail continues down from Panama all the way to Chile (with a side-route then running east through Argentina into Brazil).

A highly simplified overview of the South America Gringo Trail (showing some of the major stops only)

If you want to combine this route with the one in Central America, it's important to note that overland travel between Panama and Colombia is not possible, and so these routes do not connect directly. Instead, many backpackers will either fly across or sail around it by private charter boat.

Colombia used to be frequently skipped by travellers during the 'bad days', but it is increasingly becoming a key part of the Gringo Trail as its security situation has improved dramatically over the last few years. The trail continues down into Ecuador, Peru, Bolivia, Chile and then tapers off into either Argentina or Brazil. The Atlantic side of South America is much less travelled (with countries like Suriname or French Guyana barely visited at all), and the vast majority of backpackers travel along the Pacific side through the aforementioned countries. You will find backpacker hostels, low-cost hotels, and the usual tourist infrastructure all along this route.

The same disclaimers regarding language apply as with Central America: it helps to know some Spanish. Travellers in South America will also need to be a little sensible when it comes to security, as crime can be a problem in some parts (in particular in capitals and bigger cities).

Distances can be huge in South America and so you should be prepared for some long journeys. Spending 12 or 15 hours in a bus is commonplace. Once you get to Argentina and Brazil, distances will get particularly crazy, with some laps between key waypoints reaching nearly 24 hours. With few budget airlines in South America, long-distances buses are still often the most obvious transportation option.

There are many major attractions along this route, including the Inca ruins of Machu Picchu in Peru, the salt flats of Uyuni in Bolivia, and the humongous waterfalls of Foz do Iguaçu on the Argentinian-Brazil border. Many will want to take a trip into the Amazon rainforest in Colombia, Peru, Bolivia or Brazil.

The further south you go, the more developed and modern the countries become—with prices to match. While Ecuador, Peru and Bolivia are extremely cheap, Argentina, Chile and Brazil are relatively costlier.

East Coast Australia

Challenge Level: *Easy*

Typical Length: *1 to 2 months (more on a large budget or if on a working holiday)*

Australia is a big, big country—which is why the typical backpacker route here runs mainly along the more populated east coast (and also, of course, because much of the inland areas consist of barren desert).

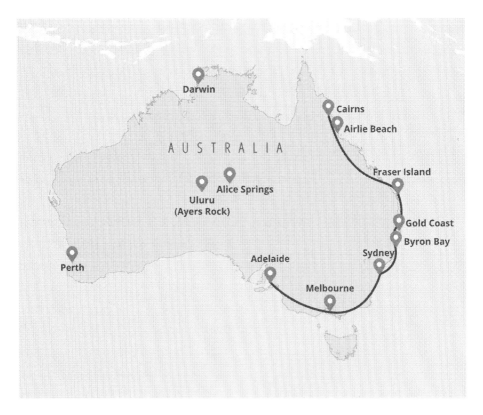

The route starts in Adelaide or Melbourne, then works its way up to Brisbane and then finally to Cairns in the northeast, stopping at various smaller places along the way—often including places like Airlie Beach, Noosa National Park, Byron Bay and Fraser Island. While the east coast forms the spine of the Australia backpacker trail, many will also want to make excursions into other parts of the continent, such as exploring the outback and visiting Uluru (Ayer's Rock).

One of the most popular ways to get around is by Greyhound public bus. For the more adventurous, campervan hire allows additional flexibility as well as mobile accommodation. This is a popular option even with travellers who ordinarily use public transportation, as not having to pay for accommodation as well can help keep costs down.

Australia is not cheap. Accommodation costs, food, and transportation are all pricey compared to other parts of the world. Multi-day activities and tours can feel like major investments, typically costing hundreds of dollars each. Cooking your own food and using other cost-saving methods are recommended if you wish to travel longer in Australia on a limited budget.

While not always so easy on the wallet, Australia does have the perfect combination of being quite exotic (to the non-Ozzie, of course) and quite familiar all the same, as there are few major cultural barriers or travel challenges to deal with. Kangaroos and koalas can sure make you feel like you're in a different world, yet the country functions not so differently from North America or Europe.

Since travelling in Australia is pretty easy, it does attract a somewhat younger backpacker crowd on average, so don't be surprised to encounter more wide-eyed 18-year old travellers in hostels than you might elsewhere (if this is your demographic, you will of course feel right at home). That said, like any other destination, Australia does see travellers of all ages. If you are looking for an excellent starter country and don't mind the expense, Australia is a great choice. Australia is often combined with New Zealand, which also has a well-trodden backpacker trail from north to south, running mainly between Auckland and Christchurch.

Finally, Australia is legendary as a working holiday destination. Well-paid temporary or seasonal work is easily found here, and so it has become somewhat a refuge for travellers looking to top up their bank accounts. Jobs commonly include farming or fruit picking, restaurant/service jobs, and au pair jobs. Australia is very flexible with issuing working holiday visas, and so many backpackers come from South-East Asia down to Australia to work for a while before heading on elsewhere.

The great European city trip

Challenge Level: *Easy*

Typical Length: *1 to 3 months*

Europe is the odd one out in this list as it doesn't have as clear of a route. Whereas routes in Australia or South America have just two ways to go—up or down!—Europe is a wide open mesh of cities that can be navigated in many different ways.

Do you focus on the northern circuit of London, Paris, Amsterdam and Berlin? Do you head down south into Bordeaux, Madrid, Barcelona, Nice, Florence and Rome? Do you dive into the Alps, or hit up more of Middle- and Eastern Europe with cities like Krakow, Prague and Budapest? There are simply countless ways to make your way through the continent.

Trips through Europe tend to focus on cities, which is not surprising given the incredible history and cultural depth you can find there. Nevertheless, there are countless outdoors experiences outside of the cities that are also not to be missed (if you can fit them into a no doubt already tight schedule).

One of the great ways to travel Europe is by rail. The rail network is fantastic throughout the continent, and so an attractive option for a big trip is to get an Interrail pass (www.interrail.eu) if you are a European citizen or a Eurail pass if you are from outside the EU (www.eurail.com). These flexible passes let you make a big whistle-stop tour of Europe all for one combined price. Some packages let you explore all of Europe by train without limits, while cheaper packages let you cherry-pick the countries you want to travel through. There are special discounts if you are under 25.

While there isn't one specific route through Europe that everyone follows, many European trips do start in London due to the many flight connections to Heathrow, and with Paris just 2 hours away by train you can have an exciting start to your trip. The most obvious routes snake their way through France, Spain, Italy, Austria, Switzerland and Germany, The Netherlands and Belgium—basically drawing a wide circle around the Alps in the middle—though there are countless other ways through Europe.

Travelling in Europe is not cheap. If you're on a budget, be prepared to hack it at least to some degree. You might have to pack your own lunches, look for freebie activities (like free city walking tours), and so on. Camping, hitch-hiking and couchsurfing can help you travel Europe on a shoestring budget.

If you want to stay in Europe longer or on a lower budget, head east. The Balkan coastline will remind you of countries like Italy but at far lower prices (except perhaps for Croatia, which is getting more expensive—especially Dubrovnik which featured heavily in *Game of Thrones*). The Baltic states are relatively less travelled (apart from Fins and British going on quick weekend trips) and remain very affordable. In Budapest you can just smell the comings and goings of empires through the ages, yet it's remarkably inexpensive compared to the capitals on the rest of the continent. Similar things can still be said about Prague, as well. Head all the way south-east, to Romania, Serbia, Albania, Bulgaria, and Ukraine, and you can still travel on budgets of around $30 a day—closer to prices in Southeast Asia than those in Paris or London. Beware of prices in the Nordic countries and in Switzerland however, as these have some of the highest travel costs in the world.

The so-called Schengen visa provides up to 3 months of travel within 26 European countries, so Europe trips usually max out at 3 months. Travel in Europe is generally easy, with few cultural or language barriers, excellent public transport, and high levels of safety. Europe trips are especially popular as a summer trip for college-age Americans, though you can meet travellers of all ages and nationalities all along the many backpacker trails.

India (and South Asia)

Challenge Level: Hard (India), Easy / Moderate (Sri Lanka, Himalayas/Nepal)
Typical Length: 1 to 3 months

India is a tough nut to crack, demanding some patience and determination from travellers. You may be overwhelmed by sensual overload and constantly dealing with attention from touts or curious crowds. Stomach issues are par for the course, and getting a case of the "Delhi belly" seems almost unavoidable.

Then again, many a traveller returns from India with a glint in their eye, feeling like they've truly visited another world. It is ultimately a country of extremes, one that can be very stressful at times but uniquely rewarding as well. India remains one of the quintessential overland backpacking destinations—a fascinating and diverse country, with vast differences in geography, climate, culture, language and ethnicity.

While there are many different regions within India, and while you could spend multiple trips just getting to know each part, there is a clearly identifiable 'backpacker route' through much of the country. Many will hit up Kerala and Goa in the south-west, move up to Mumbai, then focus mainly on Himachal Pradesh and destinations in the surrounding states, then onwards to Agra, Varanasi, with finally a possible crossing into Nepal. That's not to say there's not a lot more to India than these places, but this (already quite huge) route forms the spine of many people's itineraries.

There's a stereotype of people coming to India for spiritual reasons or to "find themselves". Certainly this stereotype holds true to some degree, and so you will find that some are in fact in India on a bit of a personal quest. In contrast to the younger backpacker vibe in Southeast Asia, the India traveller crowd is spread out further across the entire age range, including a greater share of older travellers as well.

If going to India, be sure to prepare well, and check the climate so you can avoid the hottest periods of the year. There are also some controversies around female solo travel in India that may be worth looking into (some argue that India is not a very safe or welcoming place for solo female travellers, though others argue this isn't the case so as long as you know what you're doing).

If you have little or no prior travel experience under your belt, you might want to level up your skills somewhere else before going to India. Ultimately, India is not *that* much different from travelling anywhere else in the developing world, but since everything tends to be turned up to 11, you might want to hit up an easier place at first.

Nearby Sri Lanka and Nepal are sometimes combined with a trip to India. Sri Lanka is often billed as "India, but less crazy"; culturally it can feel somewhat similar, but travelling here is a lot easier and less hectic. Nepal is one of the world's most popular destinations for mountain trekking, with countless routes running through the Himalayas. Even those not interested in hiking might want to pay a visit to Kathmandu (as there is more to Nepal that just the mountains).

Southern & Eastern Africa (Garden Route and beyond)

Challenge Level: *Easy / Moderate (South Africa) to Moderate / Hard (elsewhere)*
Typical Length: *1 to 2 months, or more depending how far north you go*

Africa is a huge continent that's home to over 50 countries. That makes it hard to generalise, and my personal experience with the continent is limited, though broadly speaking it is not known as an easy continent to travel. Transport infrastructure is often poor and unreliable, and while there some notable exceptions, most countries lack the sort of convenient accommodation and travel facilities that make other parts of the world much easier to deal with. Many iconic travel experiences in Africa are surprisingly expensive, as African tourism has specialised mainly in attracting short-term holidayers willing to pay large sums for well-catered safaris.

Specific individual countries do often make the lists of popular budget destinations, such as Morocco and Egypt in the north, or Ethiopia in the east. Though as far as well-travelled overland routes go, there is really one: the Garden Route through South Africa, which is increasingly extending into nearby countries including Zimbabwe, Mozambique or Tanzania (including Zanzibar).

South Africa is very much a backpacker country in the same sense that places like Central America or Australia are, and this makes it a good entry point into the continent. South Africa is full of backpacker lodges, and transportation is easy, including a hop-on-hop-off backpacker bus service running all along the coast. It's one of the cheapest developed countries to travel, though many will of course say it's not quite the "real" Africa from a cultural point of view—for that you will have to cross the border into any of its neighbouring countries.

Besides many national parks, South Africa is increasingly known as an adventure sports destination (with popular activities being wakeboarding, windsurfing, skydiving, shark cage diving, and so on). The crime rate is high in South Africa and Johannesburg is particularly problematic, so many visitors do tend to spend more of their time elsewhere in the country. The popular so-called Garden Route runs roughly from Cape Town along the coast up to Johannesburg, or potentially onwards across the border into Mozambique or Zimbabwe.

The further you get away from South Africa, the more things can turn into a bit of a mission—either due to getting increasingly off-the-beaten-track, or because of budget pressures. For instance, going to iconic places such as Kilimanjaro and the Ngorongoro Crater in Tanzania, while thrilling, is not exactly cheap once you have to start paying for tours or safari packages.

Other routes

This list is, of course, not entirely exhaustive. We haven't mentioned China yet, which is an increasingly popular backpacking destination, sometimes as an addition to the South-east Asia trail.

The United States should be noted as well, though it has much less of a backpacker or hostel culture and so, as far as long-term travel goes, it doesn't pop up on the radar quite as often. Public transit options can be very crummy, and since the US is a very car-focused country it's arguably best suited for road trips. This is not to say you can't go backpacking in the US, but it is lacking the sort of convenient and clearly defined traveller routes you find elsewhere.

Some major overland routes used to be big but have since fallen out of favour. There's the Silk Road hippie backpacker trail for instance, which used to be popular in the 1970s (and which in many ways paved the way for the culture of backpacking today). Changing geopolitical situations and the conflicts in Afghanistan and Iraq caused this route to be largely abandoned. However, the odd hardcore traveller might still attempt an alternate route through Iran, up through Turkmenistan and Uzbekistan, and then back down into India, avoiding the aforementioned trouble spots.

Then there's the Trans-Siberia Express, which can take you all across Eurasia by train, from the westernmost Russia to Mongolia and China. It's a long and somewhat lonely journey, though being the longest railway line in the world it continues to draw its share of dedicated overland travellers.

Clearly, we could go on for a while, as there are so many ways to travel the world. (And we've mainly discussed longer overland routes here, not individual countries which may of course merit a visit just on their own.) Earth is a huge place and you can, in theory, follow your compass in any direction. However, the routes covered in more detail earlier are ones that are more established and more frequently travelled. If you're looking for well-tested and accessible overland journeys, they're the first ones to look into.

Inspiring travel TV shows

I often get ideas for future trips from watching shows and documentaries about travel. The following ones are among the best around: watching them is guaranteed to fill your heart with pure wanderlust...

Departures

While sometimes a little thin on information, this show gives you a great feel for what backpacker travel can be like. It's just two hosts and one cameraman going on adventures around the world, meeting random people along the way, and constantly getting into unscripted and unexpected situations. While originally produced for Canadian TV, it has now been released worldwide on Netflix, where it has gained a cult following. This show can give you some great travel ideas, and might well inspire you with its fun sense of camaraderie.

Parts Unknown

A breathtakingly filmed, extremely well-researched and Emmy-award winning show by former chef and professional traveller Anthony Bourdain. *Parts Unknown* has a genuine curiosity for other cultures—what people do, what they eat, their hopes and their dreams. It will show you interesting things you've never seen, by a traveller who is, by now, a little older and wiser; a great counterpoint to the more foolish attitude of *Departures*. Airs regularly on CNN, and can be downloaded from Amazon Instant Video, iTunes and elsewhere.

Long Way Round

The ultimate road tripping inspiration. I've encountered countless motorcyclists on my travels who were directly inspired by this series. In *The Long Way Round*, actors Ewan McGregor and Charlie Boorman decide to ride around the globe on motorcycles—going through Europe, Russia, Mongolia, crossing the Bering strait and finally riding through Canada and the US. The resulting mini-series is raw and riveting, and will make you want to grab a motorbike and hit the road. A follow-up, *The Long Way Down*, takes the pair down from Europe into Africa, and is equally worth watching. Available on DVD, Hulu, Netflix, and elsewhere.

Road trip or public transportation

Using public transportation (e.g. buses, trains, taxis, auto-rickshaws, and so on) is generally the most accessible and hassle-free way to move around. Many backpackers rely on public transport connections exclusively, and most big trips are done in this way.

One downside to using public transport is that you are sometimes limited in where you can go. Travelling as a passenger is easy when following the at least somewhat beaten track, but going to less-explored parts can be challenging without having your own vehicle. When I'm backpacking the traditional way, I too sometimes wish that I could just jump into a car and go entirely my own way.

If you mostly travel by public transportation, you may still find some good opportunities to use your own vehicle for specific laps of your journey. For instance, it's popular to travel Vietnam north-to-south or vice versa by motorbike, as it's very cheap and easy to either rent or purchase a motorbike here. In Australia and New Zealand, many backpackers rent camper vans for increased mobility and for having a 'free' place to sleep. In Africa, renting a vehicle is often a necessity, as countries here frequently lack the sort of public transportation networks that make backpacking the other continents so much easier.

If you are thinking of doing your *entire* journey as a road trip, know that this takes a lot of additional preparation and dedication, especially if you are planning to go road tripping in any countries where road quality and services aren't exactly optimal.

It helps to know something about basic car or motorbike repair, and it's a good idea to choose a brand of vehicle for which you can easily find spare parts where you are going. You will probably need to get your vehicle internationally insured. Additional paperwork is often required at borders, as your vehicle may need to be cleared by customs. Be sure to get good accurate maps as well. This cannot be stressed enough: what looks like a highway on a road map of, say, Guatemala may in fact be the narrowest dirt road you've ever seen (just speaking from experience here...). Shipping a vehicle across oceans can be very challenging, so while some adventurers try to circumnavigate the globe by car or motorbike, this isn't necessarily straightforward.

Bear in mind that driving in the more remote parts of the world can be tiring: you will often need to keep an eye out for goats, donkeys, potholes, unmarked speed bumps, and so on. Compared to using public transportation, you will get less downtime and less opportunities to catch some sleep between destinations.

That said, there is also something truly wonderful about going on a road trip. You connect with the landscapes of a country so much more. You are under less pressure to pack light, making it easier to bring your own food and camping equipment. You can get off-the-beaten-track much more easily, leading to more unique experiences. And it's not just the sights that make such a journey worthwhile, but also the constant process of way-finding and problem-solving along the way.

This book is mostly about travelling long-term using public transportation, but it's worth mentioning at least a couple of popular long-term road trips.

Firstly, there's Route 66 in the U.S., long considered "America's most famous road". While this highway actually no longer exists in its original form, the idea of the classic America road trip lives on in the popular imagination. Various alternate coast-to-coast U.S. road trips still evoke the original spirit of Route 66: search for "Route 66 alternatives" online for specific ideas. (Obviously, roads in America are of better quality than in the scenarios painted earlier.)

Then there's the Pan-American Highway. This surely has to be the ultimate road trip, as it runs from the Patagonia region in the southernmost tip of Argentina all the way up to Alaska along the pacific coast of the Americas. This route doesn't have to be followed for its entire length, of course. Some focus only on the Latin America section of the trip, which is a route that also happens to roughly match the popular backpacker Gringo Trail detailed earlier. You can find a wealth of information (including such issues as how to deal with corrupt police) at www.drivetheamericas.com.

Another popular long-distance road trip is the Eurasia route running roughly from Istanbul in Turkey to Ulan Bator in Mongolia, via countries such as Uzbekistan and Turkmenistan. This route has gained much attention in recent years as it is host to an annual informal event called the Mongol Rally, in which anyone can participate. The goal of the Mongol Rally is to drive a deliberately small and/or decrepit car from Europe or Turkey all the way to Mongolia, while raising money for charity. You can find more information at www.theadventurists.com/mongol-rally

This only scratches the surface, of course. A good general resource for road travel is the wiki located at www.wikioverland.org, which has specific road tripping information on 50+ countries and has much advice on all of the practical issues you will face.

While road trips can be exciting, such expeditions are not without their challenges—and if this is your first world trip or long-term journey, you are possibly better off using public transportation.

That said, completing specific segments of a backpacking or round-the-world trip by rented vehicle requires less advance preparation, and so this can be an option to consider even when you don't have much prior experience.

Bucking the bucket list mentality

While it's good to think big, make sure you'll be able to savour your journey as well. The world is a huge place, and you could easily trip over yourself just trying to 'see it all'.

Social media can subject us to constant streams of people's selfies in front of iconic landmarks or exotic locales around the world, which can easily make us feel restless and hurried. If you're not also going to all these places, are you missing out? The me-too effect can make itineraries quickly grow out of proportion.

Bucket lists are problematic as well. In theory it's a good exercise to think about what you hope to do in your life, but bucket lists more often than not lead to tunnel vision, unrealistic expectations, or box-ticking mentality.

Pinning all your expectations on any boilerplate "achievements", or doing things merely just to say you have done them, is probably not so helpful. Maybe swimming with dolphins will be the best experience of your life, or maybe it won't. (Somehow it's always the same cliché things...) Maybe you *have* to visit all 7 continents before your die, or maybe you could happily die not having been to some of them. There are no badges or prizes for any of this, so consider if it's what *you* really want to do, or if it's just what everyone else is trying to do.

If you have a bucket list, throw it away. The most a bucket list will do for you is make you constantly feel like you haven't done everything yet, and there are better ways to channel your travel ambitions than with a list or spreadsheet.

On a more general note, it's nice to slow down. Don't try to cram 6 months' worth of travel into 3 months; it's much better to go for quality over quantity. If you find it difficult to pare down your destination choices into a more manageable plan, remind yourself that countries or places you might not have time for now are still going to be there later. With only few exceptions, there's no need to rush to every destination.

(On a side note, I am grateful to have visited countries like Myanmar and Cuba before globalisation came knocking on their doors. But such precious frozen-in-time destinations are rare, and most places will still be there for you later. For example, I haven't yet seen the Pyramids of Giza in Egypt, but I am fairly confident that, barring some kind of apocalyptic event, they will still be there for me to see in a few years' time.)

If you find yourself getting dizzy from the sheer number of possibilities for your journey, take a deep breath and remember that you can always travel the world one step at a time.

Key points from this chapter

- Think about what the **purpose of your journey** is. Knowing what you hope to achieve or get out of a big trip can help inform your planning decisions.

- **Developing countries** may be a little rougher around the edges, but they are also dramatically less expensive than the more advanced economies, which makes them excellent candidates for big, long-term journeys. If your trip is meant to be a marathon and not a sprint, be sure to consider these cheaper destinations.

- **Round-the-world trips** give you more variety, but can also be costlier and involve more planning. **Overland trips** can be more immersive and are usually less costly as well. Overlanding gives you more of a feeling of being on a continuous journey. Zipping around by plane between regions and continents will, of course, let you cover more ground.

- Going on a **road trip** requires more preparation and can be more of a challenge (e.g. dealing with mechanics, paperwork at borders, etc.). Using **public transportation** is easier, though gives you somewhat less freedom in where you can go. Most backpacker-style travellers use public transportation.

- While many travellers aspire to go totally their own way, the majority do end up travelling on **clearly identifiable circuits**. You can follow such routes while still making various detours of your own. Often such backpacker routes exist simply because they are the most sensible routes. The major ones are described in this chapter.

- While you will surely want to be ambitious with your trip, **don't over-stretch yourself.** It's a shame to go through places very hurriedly only to say you've been there. Don't bite off more than you can chew: you can always leave some countries for future trips.

[3]

Financing your travels

MONEY IS WHAT MAKES the world go round, and it is what makes you go around the world. Having dreamed big of where you want to go, now comes the harsh reality of finding the funds to do it.

People often think that you need to be extremely lucky to be able to afford a world trip. Recently I saw a poster in my local supermarket showing someone on an inflatable lounger bobbing around a tropical island, which I immediately recognized as Krabi in Thailand. It was an ad by the national lottery. It said, "PLAY MAKES IT POSSIBLE". I shook my head. I have been to that island, and spent an incredible amount of time in other wonderful places, and I never won the lottery.

It's not luck nor lotteries that make things possible, but determination and maybe some patience. If you are serious about going on a big journey and you make it a priority in your life, chances are you can get more funds together than you might have thought possible.

Personal finances are all about managing faucets and drains. There might well be some faucets that you can open a little further to increase your travel funds. An equally useful method is to look at what's draining money from your bank account and to make some adjustments in how you're spending your money.

Before you start looking at those faucets and drains however, you will need to know how big of a money reservoir you will need to fill up for your trip.

Determining a budget

To set a funding target, you obviously need to know how much money your trip will cost. But the longer your trip, the less of an exact science this becomes.

For a shorter holiday you might well book everything ahead, in which case you could put nearly every anticipated expense into a spreadsheet and get a very accurate estimation of your total costs. On a big trip you are far less likely to book everything ahead, and your whims as a traveller might lead you towards unexpected expenses (or financial windfalls) during your journey, making it more difficult to get an extremely precise budget up-front.

When estimating your budget, always assume it will be a rough ballpark estimation. Save up maybe 15 to 20% more than you think you will need, just to give yourself some room to manoeuvre. Either you will end up having some extra savings in the bank for when you get back (clearly this is never a bad thing), or it will give you some financial cushion while travelling. It's nice not to have to stress out quite as much over the occasional budget overrun or emergency expenditure. There's nothing worse than being half-way around the world in a place you're not likely to be back any time soon, and realize you can't afford something you really want to do because you are on an overly tight budget. You've already come this far and now you can't go that final mile, just because your estimations were a little too optimistic.

If you want to go balls-out with your budgeting, then you only need to look for spreadsheet templates online. Search for terms like "RTW travel budget spreadsheet" or "RTW budget calculator" and you will find spreadsheets with dozens of tabs and countless of columns that let you seemingly work everything out to the last cent. Don't let such spreadsheets deceive you into thinking you can truly predict all of your expenses, though they are very helpful tools in breaking down your overall estimate into smaller parts.

In the example ahead we are going to keep things a bit simpler. Determining a budget does not have to be rocket science: it can be as basic as making a list of your fixed or non-recurring costs and a list of your daily travel costs.

For your fixed costs, count anything you need to spend in order to start your journey, as well as the major non-recurring expenditures you expect to have (for instance an expensive ticket to see a major attraction, or a course you are planning to take somewhere). Here is a hypothetical example of some fixed costs for a 3-month trip:

Return Flight Home	$700
Backpack	$150
Extra SD Card For Camera	$30
Vaccinations	$70
Travel Insurance	$200
Travel Guide	$20
Souvenirs Allowance	$50
Visa costs	$30
3-Day Scuba diving course (special one-time expense)	$250
Misc. other / emergency cushion	$300
Total	**$1800**

Then, separately work out your day-to-day costs of living. This includes food, drinks, accommodation, and allowances for transportation and sightseeing.

Travel guides usually give a broad estimate for daily costs (e.g. "between $20 and $30 a day") which can be a good starting point. When you are relying on such daily cost estimates, make sure it's for a travel style that matches your own. For instance, some sources might say you need at least $70 a day in a particular country, but perhaps this assumes you will be staying in hotels and eating dinner in upmarket restaurants. On a backpacker budget, you might be able to do it for $30 a day. Travel guides typically have a low, mid and high range estimate for a country.

There are many example daily budgets online as well. For instance, you can find a killer list of travel budgets at www.legalnomads.com/wds#budget Again, be sure what kind of travel style these examples are based on (are they luxury travellers? Or RTW/backpacker travellers? Maybe somewhere in between?).

Another way to find your daily cost estimate for a particular country is to make one on your own by collecting bits of specific information (such as the average price of a meal in a budget restaurant or the average price of a beer). Good websites to use for this are www.priceoftravel.com and www.budgetyourtrip.com. For accommodation costs, you can look at booking sites to find out how much you will need to spend on average. Put everything in a table and you'll get a rough daily cost:

Accommodation average cost	$7
Daily food budget	$10
Bathroom supplies, other consumables	$1
Drinks/going out	$5
Transportation (overland) daily average	$4
Sightseeing budget	$5
Total average per day	**$32 / day**

If you are planning to travel through multiple countries, include a daily cost estimate for each country. Then add up your daily costs depending on how long you are expecting to stay in each country, and add up your fixed costs, and you will have yourself a rough budget.

Of course, you might end up spending longer in some countries or shorter in others, which could throw off your estimates. What you are doing right now is just setting a reasonable target. You can monitor your spending during your trip to see if you are over or under budget, and make decisions accordingly.

Saving up money

Unless you happen to already have enough savings, you will now need to save up money until you can cover your estimated budget (plus a little more, just to be safe).

The key to getting your travels funded is to make it your top priority. The more determined and disciplined you are, the faster you will get there.

Consider opening a separate savings account for your travel fund so that you can keep the money clearly separated, track your progress more easily, and better resist any urges to spend those hard-won savings.

Increasing your income

At the risk of stating the obvious, the easiest way to save up money is by making more money. Not everyone will have the same opportunities to do so, of course. But see if you can get a raise, bring in some additional clients (for instance, if you're a freelancer), or work two jobs at the same time.

Saving up will be easier if you have a well-paid high-skilled job of course, but you can still save up without one. To give just one example, I recently met a Dutch girl in Indonesia who funded a three month Asia trip just by working extra shifts as a waitress. It is common for graduates or students in particular to fund their travels through side jobs, summer jobs, or seasonal work. Countries with a good minimum wage (or where unskilled jobs are paid well) are obviously most suited to this.

Consider if there is extra work you could be doing on the side. The internet makes this increasingly easy. You can look for online jobs at sites like Upwork (www.upwork.com) or Fiverr (www.fiverr.com), for example. Browse the skills that are on offer on these platforms to get ideas for things that you can do. You can also use the sharing economy to make some extra cash. You could drive people around with Uber or Lyft, cook dinner for people with EatWith (www.eatwith.com), or become a tour guide in your local area with Vayable, WithLocals or GetYourGuide.

Let your friends and family know about your travel goals, as they may be able to help you in achieving them, for instance by alerting you to some money-making opportunities.

If your birthday or Christmas (or another holiday) comes around, you can ask them for contributions to your travel fund instead of the usual gifts.

Reducing your spending

Besides attempting to turn up those faucets, you can also look at your money drains.

It's easy to spend money when you have it, but you might not be spending it wisely right now. Many people won't blink at spending serious money on new clothes, going out, or on expensive hobbies, but it's time to de-prioritize such expenses. By examining your expenses line by line, you can also often find many little savings that can combine into significant savings over time.

Here are just some ideas on how to save up:

- **Stop buying things.** Focus on making maximum use of the things you have now instead of buying new things. Temporarily suspend buying any new clothes and make the best use of your existing wardrobe. Resist buying any new electronics or other big expenses. Stop buying new video games and play what's already in your Steam list or on your game console. If you think you need something, wait at least a few weeks before buying it—either the moment will have passed, or you'll be a little more certain that you actually need it.

- **Find a roommate (or move in with your parents).** Rent often represents a huge chunk of people's monthly expenses and so this is a prime place to look for savings. Reduce your rent by sharing your place with other people or putting a room on Airbnb. Alternatively, you can look for a cheaper place to live for a while. You can also consider the extreme option of giving up your place entirely and temporarily moving in with you parents (this may or may not be an option depending on your age or where you are in life). This is usually not an ideal situation, but you'll save up very fast.

- **Get rid of unneeded subscriptions.** If you have multiple TV or online streaming subscriptions, pare it down to just one, or only watch things that are for free for a while. Evaluate your magazine subscriptions, online subscriptions, gym memberships, or anything else that involves recurring payments that you could either freeze or cancel.

- **Downgrade your mobile plan.** Check how many of those minutes or megabytes you are actually using. Often you can get by with a cheaper plan (or with pay-as-you-go).
- **Cook more meals at home.** Go to restaurants less often, and cook at home instead of getting take-out. Cooking at home can be fun: why not try some recipes from the countries you want to travel to? Invite friends over for dinner instead of going out.
- **Brown-bag your lunch.** This takes just ten minutes every morning but can save you a bit of money every day.
- **Make your own coffee.** Cut down on those expensive cappuccinos and lattes from coffee houses. If you are in the habit of buying a coffee every morning on your way to work or uni, changing that habit can save you a decent sum on a weekly basis. You can get a French press and make your own coffee instead of buying it from a café.
- **Drink less alcohol.** Go out less frequently for a while and you can make significant savings. This can be a bit of a sacrifice, but keep your eyes on the prize. Those two cocktails that you're not having tonight might well represent an entire day's budget in Vietnam.
- **Quit smoking.** Difficult no doubt, but also unquestionably good for your health and for your wallet.

These are of course just some ideas, and you can probably think of some more that are specific to your circumstances.

Don't take your personal austerity program too far though. If you haven't left your house in months, eat only Heinz beans (purchased in bulk), and have reduced your entertainment options to playing solitaire or telling stories to your cat, you might have cut a little too deep. Making too many sacrifices can actually lead you to lose motivation. Find a balance between living modestly for a while but still allowing yourself to have some fun.

Decluttering

Another great way to make some extra money is to sell things you don't really need. It's amazing how much you can end up hoarding over the years.

Go through all of your stuff—all of it!—and be as thorough as you can. Pretend you are moving house and that you have to pack up everything: open every drawer, cupboard, and storage space, and take a full inventory of everything you own. Think hard about the last time you actually used each item, then eliminate anything that doesn't serve a clear purpose in your life. Have a yard sale or sell things on eBay, Craigslist, Gumtree, or whatever your local equivalent is.

I did this before one of my journeys and earned myself an additional month of travel. I kept digging up things that I hadn't even thought about since, well, probably the last time I moved. I sold many videos games, box sets, and movies that I was realistically not going to ever touch again. I found my old broken laptop and realized I could probably still sell it for spare parts (and it sold for much more than I expected). I sold my printer with the goal of going paperless. A bunch of kitchen appliances that I never used went out the door too.

Decluttering can not only make you an extra buck, but it can be a worthwhile exercise in its own right. As the saying goes, "the things you own will end up owning you." Now might be a good time to donate unwanted clothes to charity, or to throw out those stacks of magazines that have just been accumulating. There are many excellent blogs dedicated to having a more purposeful and minimalist life free of things you don't really need. Check out Zen Habits (www.zenhabits.com) or Becoming Minimalist (www.becomingminimalist.com).

If you intend to give up your home before you go off travelling, you will want to cut more deeply as doing so will hugely reduce your storage costs. Getting rid of some of your furniture or other big items will be particularly worthwhile: these are likely to cost more to store while you're away than it costs to just sell them and buy replacements later.

Eliminating debt

Don't take out a loan to finance your journey as it will surely come to bite you back later. It's not a good idea to go on a trip you can't actually afford.

You might have an already existing debt burden that makes it more difficult to simply drop everything and travel. The issue of debt is likely the most relevant to readers from the United States, as credit card debt, household debt and student debt are especially high in the US compared to many other countries. It's no wonder that travelling the world is often presented as a very radical life-changing move on many US-oriented travel blogs, as debt and career obligations have many people tied down.

While detailed personal finance advice is beyond the scope of this book, if you want to know more about this topic there are some excellent blogs you can read. Check out www.getrichslowly.org, www.goodfinancialcents.com, and www.manvsdebt.com for ideas on how to save up money or get your personal finances in order before you travel. The Man vs. Debt blog deals specifically with eliminating debt with the eventual goal of going on a round-the-world trip.

Reducing overhead

One of the most annoying issues that any long-term traveller will face is what to do with their place while they are abroad. Costs get out of hand quickly if you have to cover your travel expenses *and* cover your rent at home at the same time.

One solution is to rent out your place while you're away. This may actually cover the cost of your rent/mortgage and house insurance, or even make you a little profit. However, you will probably still have to move a bunch of your stuff out to make the place suitable for renting. You might also want to see if a family member or friend can keep an eye on the tenants and deal with any emergency situations that may arise. You can set up a redirect so that any mail goes to another temporary address.

Another option is to move out and give up your place entirely. This will probably feel like a drastic move, and it might not be worth it if you're going away for only a month or two. But for a big ambitious trip, the rent you'll be saving will clearly add up to a substantial amount. If there's no way of sub-letting your place, you might just have to move out and find a new place to live when you come back.

If you give up your home, you will need a secure storage space to keep your belongings. Perhaps you can make an arrangement with a family member or friend who has storage space to spare. If not, get quotes from some storage facilities in your area. Storage providers in city centres are usually not your best bet: while these provide highly flexible storage in a convenient and central location, they are usually very costly and so are more suited to short-term storage. If you're going away for a long while it's better to look for a storage facility somewhere outside of the city, as often they are dramatically cheaper for longer-term storage. Storage fees are a continual drain on your finances while you are away, so it is definitely worth making the effort to minimize those fees.

Make sure the storage costs don't exceed the cost of the items you are storing. If they do, try to downsize by throwing away unused items or donating them to charity, or selling items that you can easily purchase again. You truly don't realize how much things you own until you are trying to cram them all into a storage unit!

Besides rent, there might be other major overhead expenses that you'll want to avoid while you are away. For instance, think of any subscriptions you won't be needing and cancel them. Many online services allow you to freeze your account temporarily.

Working while travelling

A final way of financing a trip is to not finance it all ahead of time, but to work during your trip as well. If you ever wondered how some people can stay on the road for a *very* long time, it's usually by making an income while they travel.

Working locally

There are all sorts of ways in which you can work while travelling.

Many travellers will work in bars or do reception work in hostels. This doesn't always pay very well, and in some cases doesn't pay at all (some hostels merely offer a free bed and a meal in exchange for your labour). But if you can find a good bar or hostel gig, it can certainly help you save on your expenses or top up your bank account.

If you are still under 30 or so, it's particularly easy to get a working holiday visa in countries such as Australia, New Zealand, Canada, France or Ireland. This will allow you to stay in a country for a longer period of time than on a tourist visa, and it will let you officially apply for work. Australia is a particularly popular destination for seasonal work such as fruit-picking, and you can make a killing there so long as you resist spending all of your earnings within Australia (where cost of living is very high) but aim to spend it elsewhere instead.

One of the most popular and financially rewarding jobs abroad is to teach English as a second language. Becoming an ESL teacher requires getting certified (this takes about a month), though you will then be qualified to teach English classes almost anywhere. You can make serious cash in countries like United Arab Emirates, Saudi Arabia, Japan, South Korea and Taiwan. Salaries in other places are not as high (such as Vietnam, Colombia or China), but your cost of living there will be significantly lower. Not all ESL teachers are native speakers and some indeed speak it as their second language themselves.

Beyond teaching or seasonal work, think of any skills you have and how they might help you. Some people offer massages or haircuts to other travellers, or teach yoga or music classes. Others go busking or street performing.

You can make money by being entrepreneurial: I met one guy who was raking it in by organising bar crawls or movie nights for backpackers. One time I met a guy who was a good photographer, and so he offered to make high-quality photos for hotels and hostels and help them with their marketing in exchange for either money or free accommodation. He travelled through all of Central America in this way.

To find work you can look at local job boards, or you can use platforms specifically dedicated to connecting travellers with local temporary work.

r these include Working Traveller (www.workingtraveller.com), ﻴﻴ Monkey (www.jobmonkey.com), Kareeve (www.kareeve.com) and Jobs For Travellers (www.jobs4travellers.com.au). The key to getting increasingly better jobs through such platforms is to collect references. Grab whatever you can get at first, then make sure you do a great job and get a great reference, which you can then use to get better paid work next. This process is exactly the same as C.V. building at home, but on a smaller scale.

Flat broke? You can always just buy a wad of counterfeit bills, sold openly at a market in Phnom Penh...

The skills that often pay the best are ones that are difficult for companies to get locally. Social media marketing skills are pretty scarce in outer Mongolia. Just being able to speak English or another major language can often get you good temporary work, as well.

Finding temporary work can be as easy as just putting the word out there. Mention that you are looking for work to every shop owner and hotel or hostel manager you meet along the way. They might have a job for you, or might know someone else who has.

Working remotely

Another category of work takes place entirely over the internet. The last decade or so has given rise to the "digital nomad", or location-independent knowledge worker. If you have any job skills that require only a laptop and an internet connection, then this could be you. Work that you can potentially do remotely includes writing, translation, web development, search engine optimization, consultancy, accounting, marketing services, graphic design, photography, data analysis, and more.

If you are already a freelancer, then you could potentially work for your existing clients from any location. If you are already employed at a company, you may still be able to take your work from the road. I once travelled with a friend who worked for an NGO that was going through a slow period, and she persuaded her department to let her go away for 6 months so long as she would still dedicate one day a week to writing reports on her laptop.

Some digital nomads take things one step further and become internet entrepreneurs, setting up virtual businesses such as e-commerce shops, e-book sales businesses, or blogs that are monetized in various ways.

The popular manifesto for this mobile lifestyle is the book *The 4-Hour Work Week* by Tim Ferriss, which got many hopefuls chasing the dream of doing minimal work from a hammock in paradise somewhere (while mostly just travelling and having fun). This idea is of course very tantalizing, though keep in mind that nothing is quite that easy in reality.

To do this properly requires significant initial time investments. You also have to be prepared to regularly drop whatever you're doing and actually sit down and work. With no physical divides between your working day and your downtime, that can be easier said than done. You might be fully in the travel flow but then have to force yourself to find a café with WiFi or a co-working space. Digital nomads often find it very hard to get much done when they are constantly on the move, and will instead stay put in one place for a couple of months so that they can apply some focus.

Still, online work can offer great opportunities. A friend of mine travelled the world and got happily stuck living on a gorgeous volcano lake in Guatemala for a while just ghost-writing e-books for a company in the UK. I once went shark diving in the Philippines with a programmer from the US, and while we were having drinks afterwards he was simultaneously debugging a website for a client (on his smartphone, no less!). I myself managed to generate an income from my travel blog which I could update from anywhere. However, establishing a blog and gaining any income from it will take at least a year (and possibly much longer), so for most people this will not be an obvious route to funding a journey.

If you are thinking of doing just some opportunistic freelance work while abroad, check out platforms such as Upwork (www.upwork.com) and Fiverr (www.fiverr.com), which connect freelancers with all kinds of one-off jobs.

Reducing your travel costs

Having discussed how to make more money at home or during your trip, and how to save money up for your travel fund, the last potential element to making your travels more financially attainable is to actually reduce your costs during your trip.

Since this is such a big topic, it is covered in its own chapter (*See: Chapter 5. Money-saving methods*). This chapter goes into great detail on how to find cheap flights, save money on accommodation, food, and other regular expenses, how to haggle to get the best prices, and more.

Tracking your expenses

To ensure you stay on budget while you are travelling, it can be very helpful to keep close track of your expenses.

Personally, I usually already have a good idea of how much I'm spending every day on average, and my budget is flexible enough that a little overspending isn't too alarming. If you're in a similar situation, you might prefer not to think about every little bit you're spending. Instead, you can check your bank account every few weeks to see how things are tracking.

However, if you are on a tight budget, or if managing your expenses doesn't always come easy to you, keeping track of your expenses much more closely is a great idea.

Don't count on getting receipts with all your purchases as you will probably often be buying from local stores or market stalls. Your best bet is to write down your expenses in a small notebook, or to use an app on your phone to keep track.

For iOS check out Trail Wallet (www.voyagetravelapps.com/trail-wallet) or the Travel Budget App (www.travelbudgetapp.com). For iOS or Android, check out the Bon Voyage app or Conmigo. These apps allow you to set budgets, manage multiple currencies, categorize your expenses and, of course, let you check whether you've been blowing the budget or have in fact been overly frugal.

Not only can you use this type of app during your travels, they can also be a valuable tool in lowering your spending at home while you're still saving up. Seeing some actual pie charts of where your money is going can help you adapt your behaviour and find more savings in your day-to-day life.

Tracking shared expenses

Tracking your expenses is a little easier if you're solo. If you are travelling with a friend or partner, it can get a bit more complicated. Consider opening a separate account and having a shared wallet for all of your mutual food and accommodation expenses. This can be much easier than trying to work out who paid for what exactly all the time, and you can still keep other individual spending separate. Ultimately you might not be able to split things up exactly to the last cent, but if you are not too bothered by this then it's a system that works well.

There are also some apps specifically designing for divvying up expenses among multiple people. Check out Splittr on iOS, Splitomatic on Android, or Venmo on both iOS and Android.

Key points from this chapter

- **Determine a budget** so that you know how much money you will need. A budget will consist of **your fixed costs and your day-to-day travel costs**. Keep in mind that a budget can never be 100% completely accurate, especially for a longer trip, so **keep some flexibility** in your budget in case of unexpected expenses.

- You can **fill up your travel fund** at home either by making more money or by saving up. There are often lots of ways to **reduce your day-to-day spending**, either by holding off on expenditures or simply by being less wasteful. **Selling some of your belongings** can also be a great way to get some extra money.
- Try to **reduce your overhead** while you are away. Your biggest expense is probably going to be your rent: try to sub-let your place, or move out and put your belongings in storage.
- **Working while you travel** is another way for you to fund your journey and to travel longer (or even indefinitely). You can pick up the odd job locally as you travel, or you can find ways to work remotely via the internet.
- It is helpful to **track your expenses** as this will let you know how well or how poorly you are doing financially. You can use expense tracking apps in your pre-trip saving phase as well, to keep your day-to-day living expenses under control

[4]

Finding your way

YOU TRUDGE THROUGH the airport terminal in a numb haze, the halls echoing with announcements in languages you don't understand. It's been a long flight and you're tired and jet-lagged—yet you're feeling excited all the same.

This is it. This is the start of the trip you have been dreaming of. You eagerly make your way through the labyrinth of immigration checks, duty free shops and service desks, until one final hallway funnels you into the arrivals hall. As the automatic doors slide open, a new world is unlocked to you... one that you know is filled with limitless potential for adventure. You can go anywhere, do anything, be anyone!

But then you just stand there, the proverbial tumbleweed passing you by...

Uhh, right. So... what's the plan now? Where *do* you actually go from here?

All those things you hear about travelling by your own rules and just sailing with the wind might be nice and all, but they completely ignore the practical nitty-gritty of travel. How does it actually work? How do you figure out where to go, let alone where to start?

The answers may be entirely obvious and intuitive to the experienced traveller, but they can be real head-scratchers to someone planning a big trip for the first time. Many of the questions I receive from readers of my blog are about how they should actually plan their journey, or how they can deal with the basic getting-from-point-A-to-B machinations. Someone might tell me, "Okay, I know I want to travel in South America and I've been reading about it for months. But what do I do now? Do I start booking things? Do I just show up to places?"

Travelling using locals means of transportation is already half the fun (Palawan, the Philippines)

These are all good questions. Having covered the pre-trip inspiration phase earlier, let's turn our attention now to the more practical aspects of travel, such as day-to-day planning, finding places to stay, moving around from place to place, and dealing with entry visas. By learning a little bit about these topics now, you'll ensure that once you arrive at your starting destination, you won't just be paralysed by that vast horizon of possibilities ahead of you...

How to wing it with a plan

As travel writer Paul Theroux once put it, "Tourists don't know where they've been, travellers don't know where they're going." The idealized image of the drifter or wanderer is a powerful one, and many travellers will happily embrace such romantic notions of following your own path and letting the chips fall where they may.

But that may actually seem a little scary. It doesn't give you anything to hold onto. And the truth is that some planning is still required for a big journey, even if you were to play things mostly by ear.

Ideally you should plan enough to have a clear sense of what you're doing, while keeping your plans flexible enough to pursue unexpected opportunities as they come along. Striking that balance can be difficult, especially if you haven't done this before. Many travellers do unfortunately end up overplanning their trip (and as a result, wasting a lot of time and effort in their planning phase).

So what should and shouldn't you plan in advance? If you are a long-term traveller wishing to embrace the spirit of adventure, here's what I recommend:

DO research the countries you intend to go to. Find out what they're all about. Make sure you are aware of any practical challenges you may face there, any potential safety issues, the weather and climate, cultural quirks, and so on. This will let you travel with confidence and quickly hit the ground running.

DO look into visa requirements (and possibly pre-arrange visas if needed), sort out your travel insurance, and take your time to pack things well. That last point is especially important, because you'll want to pack as light as you can. (All of these topics we will get into individually later.)

DO have a broad outline in mind for the route you want to take. Maybe your plans will end up changing during your trip, but having some clear goals at the outset is very helpful.

As for what you shouldn't plan for:

DON'T start booking accommodation ahead of time, nor any transportation except for your flight to your initial starting point. Many people are accustomed to booking everything ahead before they go somewhere on holidays, but this is not advisable for longer-term independent travel. There is one exception: booking your very first one or two nights of accommodation is a good idea, as you're still just settling in and you'll probably want to know exactly where you're going after you have landed. Beyond that, it's better to take things one step at a time.

DON'T go looking for detailed restaurant or hotel recommendations before your trip has even started. It's not worth it yet, and you will probably waste a lot of time. You'll have better information on the ground, and it's much more efficient to research these things as you go.

DON'T break your whole trip down into individual days (e.g. 2 days in place such-and-such, then 3 days in place something-or-other). This might be a good idea for when you're travelling for a brief time, but you don't need to be this exact if you're travelling for many weeks or months on end. Maybe you end up loving a place, in which case why not spend 5 days there? Or 10? Maybe a place is not what you hoped it would be, and then you can simply move along. The longer your journey is going to be, the faster any such tightly wound plans will unravel.

Fear of the unknown can easily make you want to plan too much. Try to resist this urge, because winging it as you go is one of the great pleasures of long-term travel. You might want to plan your first couple of days a bit more tightly, just to get you into the flow of things. But beyond this, be sure not to box yourself in too much ahead of time.

Creating a high-level route

The longer your trip, the more you will want to look at it from a birds-eye view. Decide which countries or regions excite you the most and find some key things you want to see, but don't feel like you need to know everything exactly just yet. Planning a big trip can feel enormously overwhelming, as there are so many moving parts and so many details to get lost in. If you find yourself fretting over, say, transportation options for a part on your journey that's three months in, you should probably take a step back. Chances are that once you get closer to that part of your journey, someone can tell you exactly how to do this, or it will be easy for you to find out.

Think of your journey as a book. Imagine what kind of chapters it might have, but don't try writing all the words yet. Maybe your journey will be a trilogy: volume one will be India, volume two will be Australia, and South America the big bang finale. The chapters within them (regions, cities and places) might be clear you already, but you won't necessarily yet know how long each of those chapters will be, who the characters are, or even what the book's overall plotline will become. And that's okay. Some of things you are researching now could become part of the story, or maybe they won't, and that's just part of the fun. If you knew exactly what the entire story would be ahead of time, wouldn't that be boring?

Staying flexible

Keeping your plans flexible is generally a good idea. There are a couple of particular areas in which you might want to avoid setting too much in stone.

Pre-booked activities

You will typically find that few things require booking very far ahead, though occasionally an extremely popular activity does need to be pre-booked well in advance. Travel guides and wikis will typically call out such rare cases very clearly. For instance, hiking the Inca Trail up to Machu Picchu in Peru has become very popular and requires advance booking by at least several months. Another example of something requiring far advance planning might be a commitment to volunteer somewhere at a specific date.

If possible, put any such locked dates near the beginning of your trip, or think carefully about how much time you truly need to reach these places. Nothing is more annoying than having to rush to that fixed point on the map. Having to quickly make a beeline through several countries just to make it in time for that Inca Trail trek, for instance, can really take you out of the flow of your journey. Allow yourself ample time to get to any such pre-planned activities (or, for maximum freedom, avoid anything that needs to be locked in that far ahead).

Meeting up with friends

It's a great idea to link up with friends or family for part of your trip, or agree to meet a friend who lives locally at the destination. This does unfortunately put a stake in the ground that you cannot move. It could mean having to rush to the meeting point and abandoning travel opportunities just to make it there in time.

If possible, schedule any meet-ups or temporary link-ups with friends or family near the beginning of your trip, or keep them somewhat flexible. Perhaps your friend can agree to book a flight to a mutually acceptable destination near where you happen to be at the time. Or, if you are meeting an expat or local friend, don't lock in the dates until you know for sure when you'll be passing through the area.

The return flight

Another fixed date to avoid, at least in some cases, is your return flight. This depends on how open-ended you want your trip to be, but a one-way ticket to your initial destination is an interesting option. That way you can start your trip in one place and buy a ticket back from an-as-yet-undetermined end point. Or it lets you stay longer than you originally planned, if your finances and circumstances allow.

For this to work, keep in mind that some countries have stricter entry requirements for visitors flying on a one-way ticket. For instance, the immigration office may need to see a copy of your bank statement or a plane or bus ticket out of the country, to assure them you won't be staying illegally or won't be trapped without a way home. Check the immigration rules of your starting country to see if this is the case, as it varies per country. Sometimes the easy solution for this is to book the cheapest possible bus or train you can find out of the country, and present your booking to immigration. Bizarrely, this is typically sufficient proof that you won't be overstaying your visa.

Why your plans will change

There is a lot to be said for planning things a few steps at a time while you are travelling, instead of doing all of your planning at home. If you do get into detailed planning ahead of your trip, bear in mind that those plans will inevitably be flawed in some way and could easily change somewhere down the line.

Firstly, it's easy to be overconfident in what you can achieve in a particular timeframe. I remember this well from planning a 2-week backpacking through Peru with a friend a few years ago. We had prepared an itinerary while we were still at home, sitting comfortably in our local pub drinking cold beers with our laptops and travel guides out. In that kind of setting, looking at a route on Google Maps can easily make you shrug and think it's all going to be easy. What you don't imagine then is that taking this route involves sitting in a cramped bus for hours while getting boiled alive by the desert sun. That trip was, in hindsight, far too ambitious given the time we had.

You are also acting on imperfect information. What will the weather be like? You can't know precisely. How will you feel 8 weeks into your journey? It's impossible to say. Maybe you'll be extremely tired at that point, or maybe you will still be as hungry as at the start of your trip. Maybe some small things will go wrong along the way, like missing a transit connection or getting sick, forcing you to adapt your plans.

You won't know what opportunities will present themselves. If you plan less in advance, it becomes easier to adjust your pace, and you will constantly find opportunities to embrace spontaneity. You can take little detours to interesting places, synchronize your plans with other travellers you meet, or just stay a day longer when you feel like it. You might get unexpected invitations, learn of exciting places you had never even heard of before, or discover some brand new obsessions (maybe you get super into rock climbing, or maybe you take some surfing lessons and discover a new calling in life...)

Your plans will undoubtedly shift, and that's perfectly fine. A high-level plan is very useful, though be prepared for any of the little details to potentially change.

Choosing the best time to travel

Besides figuring out *where* to travel, another big question is when.

Most countries have high and low seasons, often coinciding with the weather during particular times of the year. Travel guides can tell you when it is the best time to visit a country, but know that you can still have a great trip outside of the 'best' months. If you are travelling long-term, it can actually-ly be an impossible puzzle to be in every country exactly at the best time.

I recently got an e-mail from someone trying to find the optimal time to follow the Gringo Trail from Mexico to Argentina (or vice versa). He sent me a whole spreadsheet of all the supposedly best times to travel in each country, along with key festivals and other dates he wanted to hit along the way. "Can you help me figure this out? It's giving me headaches!", he wrote. While I really wanted to help, it was obvious that there was simply no perfect solution to his puzzle.

This is a common stumbling block. Trying to be everywhere at the supposedly best time can be like trying to ram a square peg through a round hole. On a longer trip, the reality is that you will often have to compromise in some way.

The good news, however, is that you don't need to be so hung up on going to every country exactly in peak season. Very broadly speaking, there are often 3 months in the year that the weather is quite bad, 6 months in which it's basically fine, and 3 months in which it is meant to be ideal. Try to aim for anywhere in the latter 9 months and you will already be doing well.

In the shoulder or low season, accommodation may be easier to find and a little cheaper. The weather might not be 100% perfect constantly, but if you are spending a lot of time there anyway, there will be less of a risk than if you are spending only a week. You can deal with a few consecutive rainy days if you're in a country for a month overall, but if you only had seven days total you may feel that nearly half your holiday got ruined.

Most tropical countries have a rainy season, but this doesn't necessarily mean it rains all the time. Tropical rain showers are usually intense but short-lived. You can take shelter for an hour and wait for it to pass, and if you get wet, the sun will dry you very quickly. The landscapes will look more lush and green, though you might not have sunshine all day or every day—so everything really has its pros and cons.

Some countries also have a typhoon or hurricane season, and in this case it is a good idea to either visit outside these times or at least to keep a close eye on weather reports. Travelling in the rainy season can still be manageable, but getting stuck in a severe tropical storm is definitely unpleasant.

Travelling out of season can sometimes give you a more unique experience. For instance, cities can still be very nice in winter. Most travel guides advise you to visit, say, Prague or Vienna in summer, but they have an amazing Christmassy atmosphere in the winter months, which can give you a very different yet equally valid experience in those places.

How to use travel guides

Travel guides are the classic method of gathering trip information. You'd think they would be an anachronism in our digital age, where a world of information is constantly at our finger tips, yet they've remained a vital tool in many a traveller's tool-belt. Not only can they give you the kind of in-depth take that a quick blog post or hastily compiled 'top places to see' listicle cannot, but you can always use them regardless of whether you have an internet connection (either because you have the trusty old paper version, or because you have a digital version stored on your phone or computer).

Lonely Planet guidebooks have long been the budget traveller's favourite. Older travellers may fondly remember their celebrated black-and-white editions, which still exuded some of the original hippie spirit of its founding authors. More recently, Lonely Planet has been under criticism for going increasingly glossy and upmarket, and in recent editions you are as likely to find recommendations for $150/night resorts as for quaint family-run guesthouses. Rough Guide is often mentioned as an alternative to Lonely Planet, and their guides seem to be rising in popularity.

While undeniably useful resources, travel guides do excel at painting a rose-tinted picture. This can lead your imagination into overdrive, which can be fun... as long as you can manage your expectations.

Right now I have a Lonely Planet guide for Morocco in my backpack. It paints beautiful scenes, speaking of fertile plains, royal dynasties, and ancient caravan routes. Cities are described as an "assault on the senses", and mountain villages have a pace of life that is "seductively slow". This might all be true, though you can see they have a way with words.

Descriptions are wonderfully poetic throughout. "On elegantly wrecked seafronts, sip a mint tea and gaze at the wild Atlantic coast." Hmm yeah, tell me more...

"Miles of glorious sands peppered with small fishing villages, historic ports, and fortified towns weave along Morocco's blustery coast." Oh yeah, say it just like that...

"Berbers with light robes flutter under desert skies, their dark herds dotting the rocky hillsides". Yes, whisper it in my ears...

I should probably stop here before things get out of hand. But let's be honest about what this is: it's travel porn.

And you know what? Travel porn is awesome. It lets you fantasize about exotic places and make you feel like you are already there. It makes you excited about your journey before it has even started yet, and makes you maybe aim a little higher to find what you were really hoping to find. If you squint your eyes ever so slightly, you can see these kinds of descriptions reflected in reality.

That said, some places are described in such mouth-watering terms that they couldn't possibly live up to them... or at least, not initially. When you arrive in a place for the first time, the difference between what you thought it would be and what it actually is can be a little jarring.

When you're still just surveying the place from the window of a bus or taxi, don't pass judgement just yet, as it can take a little while for your imagined version and reality to meet in the middle. The places that make the worst first impressions often end up becoming your favourites. Of course, sometimes a place is instantly and overwhelmingly amazing, but sometimes the true beauty of a place doesn't reveal itself until you have had a chance to let it all wash over you, or see all its fascinating little nooks and crannies.

Other times, guidebooks will tip-toe around what they really want to say. Euphemisms and diplomatic language will give you clues. If a guidebook says, "this remote town may not be instantly charming, but the dedicated traveller might wish to spend a day here" it is actually code for, "Umm, you know what? Don't bother."

If your guidebook is a couple of years old, needless to say the restaurant and accommodation recommendations might not be totally reliable anymore. Such listings are especially volatile in nature: prices change, owners change, and what was just recently a great place could now have lost its lustre. Simply getting listed can change an establishment completely, and ones that went downhill long ago can still coast on a one-time positive Lonely Planet review for many years. If you are using a guidebook to tell you where to sleep and eat, it's better to get a recent edition or to look up this type of information online. (Or you have to just accept that the recommendations might not be always 100% on the mark anymore.)

Guidebooks are great for your initial research, and can come in handy in a pinch during your travels as well. Don't feel as though you can never veer off from what the guidebooks recommend though. Sometimes the best places are ones that haven't been listed anywhere yet.

Online planning resources

Besides guidebooks, you can find a wealth of travel information online. Think of the following resources not just as ones you use before your trip, but ones you can consult *during* your trip as well. They can help you with your high-level planning, but equally you can consult them on a day-to-day basis, perhaps while you're figuring out your plan for the day while sipping that morning coffee at your hostel.

1. WikiVoyage

WikiVoyage (www.wikivoyage.org) is hands down the first website you need to know about. Essentially it is the Wikipedia of travel, and has grown to become by far the most exhaustive source of free travel information. Unlike commercial travel guides, WikiVoyage can at times be a little inconsistent as it relies on user contributions only, and some less-travelled destinations get little coverage. But these are only minor complaints.

WikiVoyage is particularly great for finding general information about places, i.e. what's there to see and do, how to get there, and so on. It can also be good for finding places to sleep or eat, though dedicated booking sites can

 ~~be a little~~ better for this, as these usually have user ratings and more up-to-date details.

There is another similar site called WikiTravel, though this is a commercial version with lots of advertisements, and despite still regularly showing up in search engines it has been largely abandoned by the travel community due to problems with its management. WikiVoyage is the non-commercial version that's supported by the same non-profit organisation as Wikipedia. It now has the best information, as well as photos and maps that you won't find on WikiTravel.

Make your own travel guide

WikiVoyage has an amazing though easily overlooked feature allowing you to compile entries into your very own customized travel guide. In the sidebar, click "Create a book". Then for any WikiVoyage entry you wish to include, click "Add this page to your book" at the top of the page. You can then view your book, download it as a PDF complete with book layout, or have it sent to you as a physical book through a print-on-demand service (typically for around $10, depending on how many pages there are). If you want to save just one page, you can also click "Download as PDF" in the sidebar of any entry.

2. TripAdvisor

TripAdvisor is a commercial aggregator of travel information, offering advice and reviews contributed by users. It is a particularly useful tool for finding hotels and restaurants. The site also has a 'Top Things To Do' page for countless destinations around the world, with sights and activities sorted by user rating.

TripAdvisor ratings are taken particularly seriously by hotel and restaurant managements in some parts of the world. A few times I have sat in restaurants next to enormous human-sized signs proudly showing off their "Certificate of Excellence" from TripAdvisor.

The site is not necessarily targeted at independent travellers but at tourists in general, which can skew the ratings a little differently. It also means that a lot of the listings are in the mid or high-budget range, so it's not necessarily always best for finding those affordable local gems you may be looking for on a budget. Fortunately, you can filter by price range to narrow down your searches.

The overall composite ratings are generally very useful, but it's worth having a look at the reviews themselves to see what kind of people posted them and what their exact complaints are (if there were any). You will sometimes find reviews by spoiled tourists complaining that a low-budget hotel doesn't offer room service or an ironing board, and unfairly slapping them with a 1-star rating. I once stayed in an absolutely magical tree-hut hostel where you could literally live among a family of wild gibbons and watch the forest canopy from a sunset deck. It still had a terrible rating on TripAdvisor due to some people expecting porters to take their luggage up, or guests being aghast to find a biological toilet (in the middle of a remote jungle, no less).

TripAdvisor is a great tool to use, though the user reviews might not always be on the same wavelength as yours. Use it for finding out what's out there, but bear in mind that the ratings come from all sorts of people with wildly varying expectations—many of them on holidays with high expectations for luxury or convenience.

3. Lonely Planet Thorn Tree

The Thorn Tree (www.lonelyplanet.com/thorntree) is an online discussion board on the Lonely Planet website that's been around since the heydays of the internet. It's an excellent place to go if you have specific questions about your journey that a web search will not answer.

This forum has been around since the mid-90s. Many of the regulars in this community seem to be older veteran travellers and expat types in their 40s and 50s who have been around the block a few times. They will surely groan if you're the umpteenth person to ask about, say, "some fun stuff to do in Bangkok". But if you have a targeted question about, say, a transport connection, tips for local guides, budgeting, border crossings, security situations, and so on, you will probably get an answer here within hours if not minutes.

4. Reddit

The brainy and knowledgeable community at Reddit is also great for getting all kinds of personal pointers and advice. The subreddits /r/travel and /r/backpacking are excellent resources for both general travel tips and destination-specific information. /r/travel also regularly nominates a Destination of the Week, and by looking up these country-specific threads in the archives you can unlock a wealth of information.

Depending on your trip, other useful subreddits include /r/shoestring, /r/solotravel, /r/roadtrip, /r/languagelearning, /r/couchsurfing, and many others.

5. Nomadic Matt's Forums

This is a relatively new community having started only in 2015, yet it's already attracted a large number of travellers sharing tips and advice. Matt Kepnes' travel site is focused heavily on an American audience, so his community forums (http://forums.nomadicmatt.com/) tend to be a little more US-centric. Given that Nomadic Matt is currently the biggest travel blog on the internet, the forums are sure to grow into a huge resource in the years to come.

Ask specific questions

When using online communities to get information, always be specific. Amazingly, some will barge in with a zero-effort post like, "hey there, i'm just a regular guy going to thailand. Any tips??? thnx!". Clearly, they get few or no useful replies. Try to think of specific questions instead, write a descriptive title for your post, and include some context for people to work with (such as when you're going to be there, who you are, what your budget is, or what your interests are). If it's obvious that you have already attempted some research of your own, and that you are genuinely looking for some specific guidance, people are much more inclined to help you out.

6. Hostelworld and Hostelbookers

Staying in hostels instead of hotels can save you a lot of money, and they are amazing places to meet other travellers as well. (The exact pros and cons of staying in hostels are covered in the next chapter.)

If you are looking to book a hostel, look no further than these two sites. While hostels are rarely featured on hotel booking sites, you can find them easily through these dedicated platforms. Hostelworld (www.hostelworld.com) and Hostelbookers (www.hostelbookers.com) are the big players, though others are trying to get in on the action as well (such as www.hostelrocket.com).

The listings here are mostly in the $5 to $25 a night range. Despite what their names suggest, they don't *just* list hostels, but also various bed & breakfasts, homestays, guesthouses and some low-cost hotels.

The user ratings on these sites are nearly always up-to-date and reliable. Keep an eye out for how many ratings a place has received however. For example, a hostel on Hostelworld can have a 90% rating based on just 1 review.

Want to meet other travellers? Type in the name of the place you are going to and find the highest-rated hostel. Take a look in particular at the atmosphere rating. If it's high (let's say, anywhere above 85%), this will invariably be the cool go-to hostel where you can make a lot of friends. These top-rated hostels often become meeting places even for people who are staying elsewhere.

One specific tip for using Hostelworld: many hostels do not take bookings on the same day or within the next 24 hours. So if it's midnight and you're trying to book something for the next day, most if not all hostels will be displayed as 'full'. Often they are not actually full however (they're just not taking any more reservations), so you can still try showing up in person without a booking.

7. Agoda and Booking.com

These booking sites are especially useful for finding low-to-mid range hotel options. This is not where you will necessarily find the more social backpacker hostels, but they are a good place to look for affordable hotels offering good value for money.

Unlike more upmarket players like Orbitz and Expedia, Agoda and Booking.com have lots of budget listings, as well as plenty of listings outside of the main tourist areas. As an example, at the time of writing Expedia has just one listing for the town of Vang Vieng in central Laos, and it is a luxury resort charging $110 a night (knowing Laos, it's probably the only luxury hotel in the entire region). Agoda and Booking.com each have around 80 results for Vang Vieng, with prices as low as $11 a night.

The big players like Expedia don't really want to deal with small-fry hotels as they go for the higher profit margins only, so Agoda and Booking.com are really the ones to go to for those more affordable options.

Using word-of-mouth recommendations

Despite what the previous sections might suggest, the best travel information does not usually come from guidebooks, wikis, or booking sites. By far the best sources of information are actually the people you meet while travelling.

Backpackers are typically eager to share their impressions of where they have been. Exchanging travel information is almost like a ritual: it is not just a way of sharing knowledge, but also of making new friends. Get into a habit of speaking with other travellers and always maintain a curious attitude, and you will unlock a wealth of travel information wherever you go.

What's great about word-of-mouth information is how recent it always is. Even a recent guidebook can't tell you that something is currently closed for renovation, or that a place has gone downhill recently. New discoveries will also not yet have made it into guidebooks, and there are plenty of establishments that are not yet listed on HostelWorld or TripAdvisor.

Word-of-mouth is also a very honest and personal source of information. You can easily tell from the spark in someone's eye (or lack thereof) what a place was really like. Often I've gone to places merely because there was something in the air about them, having heard little whispers all along the backpacker trail.

Of course, not every personal recommendation is equally helpful. People have different perspectives and interests after all. Determine what kind of traveller you are speaking with and whether you're on the same wavelength. Age can be a factor too: a younger traveller with less experience may be more easily blown away than an older more seasoned backpacker. Similarly, someone on day two of their trip will still be bouncing off the walls after seeing an authentic local food market, but you may be quite used to them by the time you are in month two of your trip.

Locals are also a very useful source of information, and hostel staff and café or restaurant owners are particularly good people to ask. Taxi drivers may be biased however as they often receive commission for delivering clients to particular establishments. Locals spontaneously offering you to help you find accommodation may also have a stake in this in the form of a commission, which they collect after you have checked in. This doesn't mean they won't try to genuinely find you some good accommodation (often they do), just that they won't recommend any places they won't get money from.

Expats are often the best sources of local knowledge and you should treat these people like gold. As fellow foreigners they will see things from your perspective, but as locals they will also have extensive knowledge of the area. If you meet an expat, definitely ask them for some tips.

Finding places to stay

If you've not gone backpacking before, perhaps the thought of having to find a new place to stay every few days can give you some anxiety. You might be thinking of nightmare scenarios of not being able to find a bed at all, perhaps being forced to sleep on the street while bear-hugging your backpack and fending off the homeless trying to join you for a spoon. Rest assured, such scenarios never happen, and finding a place to stay every night is something you can quickly get the hang of.

Walk around and you might find a sign like this. It could well be a dump, or might be the best place you'll ever stay at...

It is actually possible to wing it entirely. You could just show up to places without a reservation and look around for accommodation there and then. This free-styling approach is commonly associated with backpacker travel, though it might not be the approach you'll immediately want to start with. In the beginning it certainly gives you more peace of mind to book things ahead. If you do this, try to book your next stay no more than two or three days in advance, so that you do maintain some flexibility. The idea is to book things only one step at a time as you travel, not to book everything for many days or weeks ahead, or even when you're still at home.

As you gain more confidence, you might want to try free-styling it a bit more. This approach is particularly workable along the main backpacker routes, as travellers are always flowing through these places day in day out, so you know there's going to be quite a few options around. Cities that are known to be major traveller hubs often have an informal 'backpacker district' where lots of hostels and other budget accommodation are concentrated, making it easy to check a few places quickly.

The main benefit of looking around in person is that you can have a look at the rooms or beds in each place and compare your options. It will also let you find some of those really cheap and local places that aren't listed anywhere online. When you show up in person (and have the option to walk away), it might also be possible to bargain down the price.

It's always worth gathering recommendations from travellers you meet, so that you can have a couple of hostels or hotels to target. Always ask to see the room before checking in just to make sure you're happy with it. If you arrive sometime earlier in the day (i.e. closer to noon check-out time), there will of course be more vacancies than later in the day.

Winging it is easiest when you're with a group. Some people can look after the backpacks, while others can fan out and check out some places. It's also easiest when you're in a small and walkable town, or when you're targeting a popular neighbourhood in a city that you already know will have many options. Check guidebooks or ask people where most of the budget hotels or hostels are in a city and you will often get the same responses. There's Lapa in Rio de Janeiro, Khao San Road in Bangkok or Calle 30 in Cartagena... just to name a few examples of streets or areas that everyone travelling here will surely come to know.

In some of the more well-trodden places in the developing world, you might actually be greeted by dozens of touts at your bus terminal, all promoting a different hostel or hotel. Dealing with such a deluge of attention can be a little overwhelming. Just keep your cool and ignore all the shouting, see if there's a place you might like, and remember you can still walk away if the hotel isn't what you'd hoped.

There are times when the improvised approach is less advisable. Major holidays can cause lots of places to be booked out. Be mindful of Easter and Christmas, and of local festivities such as carnivals in South America or the water festivals in Asia. You can probably still find a place in a pinch, but it just might not be the best place (or it might be very overpriced).

Winging it is particularly useful for finding those inexpensive and local places that aren't really listed on the internet, but if you are dead set on going to the 'coolest' hostel in town you probably also need to book ahead. In major travel hubs there's often one or two really happening (often Western-owned) hostels where everyone wants to go, and these do fill up quickly. If arriving somewhere very late, you might also want to have a reservation (or at least have a solid plan for where to go), as it's not ideal to be roaming the streets with your backpack late at night.

Personally, I end up booking ahead about half the time and winging it for the other half. It always depends on the circumstances.

When I do make a booking (and it's not just for a night in a stopover place), I typically book for two nights, or maybe three if I already know a place is going to be worth staying longer. I like to play it by ear: if I later feel like I want to stay a few more nights, I simply extend my stay, and this is a common approach among travellers. Unless it's at the peak of high season, most hostels can easily extend your stay if you ask them a day or two in advance. So even when you're booking things ahead, you can still wing it just in terms of how many nights you want to spend there.

To summarize, there are a number of different methods for finding accommodation:

- Ask other travellers you meet along the way (and who have already been where you're going next) about good places to stay. Sometimes it's just as easy as that. Someone might tell you "oh, just turn right after the bus stop, walk 100 meters, and then you'll find an amazing little guesthouse with two friendly dogs and a lovely old lady who makes you free breakfast in the morning". That can be your plan right there.

- If you don't already have a solid lead, open up a travel guide or online resource such as Wikivoyage.org, and look at the recommended hostels or guesthouses. You can book ahead via phone or e-mail if you want to have more certainty.

- Alternatively, using the Wi-Fi at a café or in your current hostel, go to a booking site such as Hostelworld.com or Hostelbookers and reserve a bed at a hostel with a good rating. If you are already a registered user on these sites this will take only a minute. You pay a 10%

booking fee up front and the rest of the money will be paid at reception upon arrival.

- Simply head to your destination and figure things out when you get there. If the place is fairly well-travelled, you may actually find lots of locals at the bus stop or train station offering you accommodation. Prices in this case may be negotiable.

- If your backpack is not too heavy (it shouldn't be!), you can walk around and look for signs offering rooms or dorm beds.

To reiterate, if the thought of going anywhere without a reservation seems scary right now, just focus on booking things ahead one step at a time.

Regardless of whether you booked ahead or not, arriving somewhere new is always going to be ever so slightly stressful. Navigating a new place really demands your full attention, but you're usually tired from the journey and desperate for a shower, a nap, or just a cold beer. You might feel excited about being in a new environment, but also very impatient to get that bag off your back. Arriving somewhere new can be a minor ordeal, though fortunately you're never that far away from a place where you can check in, relax, and get settled in again.

Getting from point A to B

Getting from place to place might seem complicated, but it typically isn't. You can find timetables for regularly scheduled services in travel guides, at bus- or train stations, or the hotel or hostel staff at reception can help you out with this. In developing countries, you can usually find lots of little mom-and-pop travel agencies dotted around the place where you can easily get information about transit connections. Besides scheduled services, there are frequently more informal transit options as well, such as hop-on-hop-off minivan services that run along certain routes unscheduled throughout the day.

If you are in a Western or developed country, it's usually easiest to get tickets for trains and buses online. In developing countries, you might not want to bother with this. The websites are often confusing, might not be in a language you understand, or might not accept international payment meth-

ases, it's much better to just pay in cash at a travel agency, at a
...... booth, or to get the hotel reception to arrange a reservation for you.
(Often, it isn't possible to book things online at all anyway.)

Here is a quick rundown of the types of transportation you could end up
using:

Planes: an expensive alternative to travelling overland, though low-cost
airlines can be a great option for covering more ground. North America, Europe and Asia have fantastic low-budget carrier networks in particular. Rya-
nair and Easyjet are huge in Europe, AirAsia and Jetstar are huge in Asia, and
JetBlue and Spirit Airlines are huge in North America. Africa, and Central-
and South America sadly lack such prominent low-budget carriers with large
networks, and so domestic or regional flights tend to be more expensive
here.

Buses: wherever you go chances are there'll be buses, and so this becomes
the primary mode of transportation for many travellers. The quality of service will depend hugely on where you are. In some countries, buses seemingly have no suspension and are barely able to drive up a hill (though this does
have its charm). Arrival times for these types of buses are often more than a
little optimistic; expect a long journey to take 2-3 hours longer than stated.
Maybe it does miraculously arrive on time, but it's better not to count on this.

On the other hand, buses are extremely comfortable and even luxurious
across many parts of Latin America, probably because there are fewer airlines there. Book a first class seat (still quite affordable) and you may feel as
though you are travelling by private jet, complete with 'in flight' entertainment systems and a row of attendants in formal uniforms welcoming you
aboard.

Boats: you may have to take ferries or water taxis from time to time, especially if you plan on going island hopping anywhere. Boats are not usually the
most obvious mode of transportation for longer routes (as they are rather
slow), though some specific boat trips are extremely popular with travellers.

The 2-day Mekong river slow boat in Laos, the 5-day sailing trip between
Panama and Colombia, or the 4-day boat trip from Lombok to Flores in Indonesia are just some examples of boat trips that are very popular with the

backpacker crowd. Another iconic (though considerably more arduous) boat trip is the 5 or 6-day trip from Peru to Brazil by riverboat through the Amazon.

One of the great things of being on a boat is that when you're stuck with a bunch of other passengers for a while, you inevitably get to know them well. While generally quite slow, boat trips can be absolutely phenomenal for making new friends (solo travellers, take note!).

Minivans: you can often find private minivan services throughout the developing world. Sometimes these are used by locals, other times these are specifically geared towards tourists, connecting popular tourist destinations only.

Minivans are possibly the worst way to move around. Don't be surprised if they manage to cram up to 20 people into a van that would normally seat 8. You'll have barely any legroom, and the suspension will be so bad that everyone gets constantly tossed around like a salad. If you have to go up a windy mountain road in a minivan, you might well get sick from all the swerving back and forth.

While not so comfortable, often minivans are unavoidable as there might not be any other easy options. Minivans are by far the most tolerable for shorter 2 to 3 hours rides, and on such shorter routes they can actually be faster than other options (as they'll have much more departure times to choose from than larger buses, or they are able to drop you off exactly where you need to be and not just at the central bus terminal).

Trains: A delightful way to travel. There's a kind of romance to train travel that's impossible to beat. You get plenty of leg room, you can move around the cabin if you want, and you can daydream while the landscape passes you by. Sleeper trains are brilliant, and as long as you don't mind that steady kathunk-kathunk of the wheels you can actually get you some solid sleep at night.

Europe is arguably the best continent for train travel as it has the biggest rail network, and so trains are well worth considering here.

Some particular train rides around the world are simply exhilarating. Taking a train in Myanmar is an unforgettable experience for example; expect to be bouncing all over the cabin once the train picks up some speed (unlike with those minivans, in this case it's actually a lot of fun). Trains in India are nuts, often overflowing with passengers. In northern Mexico, an amazing journey is the Pacific Railway that passes through the jaw-dropping Copper Canyon, which rivals the Grand Canyon in the US. And then there is, of course, the Trans-Siberia Express—the longest railway connection in the world.

Taxis: Useful in particular for your journeys from an airport into the city, at least if there isn't an easy public transit connection available. Taxis are comfortable, but be wary of being overcharged. For a worldwide guide on taxis with details on fares, tips on dealing with drivers or touts, and so on, go to www.ihatetaxis.com. The site has a funny name and an overly colourful layout, but offers a wealth of information.

Metro/Subway/Overground: an extremely low-cost and comfortable option in cities that have them. There are typically day or weekend passes available providing unlimited subway travel, which is a great way to hop around a city freely.

Local transportation: one of the fun things about world travel is just to see all the different flavours of local transportation. Tuk-tuks are the most common. These small motorized tricycles are an essential form of urban transport in many developing countries. Tuk-tuks can drive you around for shorter distances at prices much lower than taxis. You see them all over South- and Southeast Asia, Africa, and Latin America, and occasionally in Mediterranean Europe when there's towns with very narrow streets.

In the Philippines you also have Jeepneys, which are former US Army Jeeps converted into local pick-up buses. Sometimes golf carts are used on smaller tropical islands where the roads are too narrow for bigger vehicles. All over Central America you'll find so-called chicken buses, which are converted former US school buses, often very colourfully painted or decorated. If you're lucky, you might get on a chicken bus with a big sound system and disco lights, and where the driver doubles as a DJ...

It's fun (and inexpensive) to take these local forms of transportation, and they can really help you immerse in the local culture. Do always keep an eye on your belongings when travelling in crowded local buses.

Personal transportation: while most backpackers travel by public transportation, it is clearly also possible to travel with your own car or motorbike. Having your own transportation lets you more easily explore all the less-visited backwaters, see more of your surroundings, and stop anywhere and anytime you want, but it does also create many additional challenges and your overall progress may be slower. Refer to the earlier section on road trips in chapter 2 for some of the pros and cons.

Dealing with visas

If you wish to visit a country as a tourist, it's possible that you will have to get a visa. This is a permit allowing you to be in a country for a specified period of time. A visa comes in the form of a stamp in your passport or, less commonly, a small document that is stuck onto an empty page in your passport.

The terminology around visas can get a bit complicated. Many countries have electronic visa, visa waiver, or visa-on-arrival programmes that essentially provide automatic entry to many foreign passport holders. Sometimes such entry stamps are still called 'visas', though other times this is referred to as 'visa-free entry'. Not only is the wording a little inconsistent, there are also a lot of "if"s and "but"s around visas that can make the situation different for everyone.

If you have a passport from a Western country, then consider yourself lucky. Such passports allow easy tourist access to a huge number of countries around the world. With a passport from the European Union, Canada, US, Australia or New Zealand, all you often have to do is just show your passport at the border immigration desk, maybe fill out a brief form, get a stamp, and off you go. How long you will be permitted to stay will depend on the country you're visiting, generally ranging from 14 days all the way up to 90 days.

It's not always so easy, however. To visit some countries, you will have to arrange a visa prior to arrival. This is currently the case with Vietnam and Myanmar, for example. To get such a visa, you will have to apply for one at the country's embassy, either in your home country or in another country while you are travelling. There are also third party agencies and websites (like www.visahq.com) that can arrange your visa for a fee, which can be worth it if you want to save yourself some hassle.

You can find visa information in travel guides or on your ministry of foreign affairs or state department website. Another very easy way is to go to VisaHQ.com: just select where you are from and where you are going, and you will immediately get a clear answer as to your specific visa requirements.

When visiting countries as a tourist, there is always a certain maximum length of stay. If you wish to stay any longer, this is not always possible, but there are two things you can try.

One is to get a visa extension, if these are available. This requires going to an immigration office, of which there are usually many spread around the country, and paying for an extension. If a country offers extensions, there is usually a limit to the number of times you can extend.

Another option may be to leave a country briefly only to return for a new visa-on-arrival (a so-called visa run). This is a popular strategy with long-term travellers in Indonesia for instance, where the typical maximum length of stay is 30 days. By flying out to Bangkok or Singapore and coming straight back the same or the next day, they get themselves another 30 days. Visa runs are a tolerated practice in some places, though other times this little trick is discouraged; for instance, if your 90 days Schengen visa runs out when visiting Europe, you will have to wait another 90 days before you can re-enter.

It is wise not to overstay your visa. While some countries will be lenient if it is just a couple of days (for instance, Thailand is known to be quite accepting of minor transgressions, only giving you a small fine), other countries may not be so easily forgiving. I accidentally overstayed by one day in Vietnam and got into some serious bureaucratic issues at the border. It took a highly dubious payment of $80, plus signing a handwritten agreement that I "wouldn't sue anybody" about this payment, for immigration officials to let me off with a warning. The situation could have been easily avoided had I not messed up the dates. Some countries are extremely stringent when it comes to overstaying, and might have you deported or blacklisted. For your own sake, it's best to stick to the rules.

Some countries may have some additional paperwork requirements before you can enter. For instance, they might require evidence of onward travel (like a plane ticket or bus ticket out of the country) or a print-out of a recent bank statement (to prove that you have sufficient funds to leave the country). Such requirements are not hugely common, but specific countries can be extremely fussy about this (I'm looking at you, Costa Rica...).

Entering a country is not always free. Proper visas (ones you have to get in advance) almost always cost money. Visa-on-arrivals are more often free of charge, though from time to time these also still cost money.

Clearly, the situation around visas differs a lot on a case-by-case basis. Again, if you are unsure of any visa requirements, the fastest way to check this is at VisaHQ.com—as it will just take 5 seconds to find out.

Visas can be a bit of a pain to deal with, but they are a necessary evil. The only nice thing about visas is that by the end of a long trip, your passport will be full of cool stamps.

Keep in mind that a tourist visa will not allow you to work legally in the country, as this would require a work visa or working holiday visa.

Making day-to-day decisions

Travelling independently lets you experience things that you never will on an organised tour. It does also mean being responsible for all of your decisions, and that can put you in a bit of a jam from time to time.

If you hit a fork in the road, go with your gut...

You might find yourself at a juncture where there's many different options open to you: different places that seem equally appealing, or maybe just different routes for getting where you want to go next. This can feel like being on a TV game show where there's multiple doors with different prizes behind them. What door should you open? What if you pick the wrong one? You can find yourself sitting there staring at that thoroughly dog-eared travel guide, or having loads of tabs open in your internet browser, just agonizing over your next decision.

What can help in those situations is to get a second opinion from some other travellers. You can also try laying it all down, having a beer, having a sleep, and making a decision in the morning. Often the right answer will come to you.

Travel is not always easy. Sometimes it's full of little setbacks. You might miss a transit connection, arrive somewhere late and hungry, not sleep properly because of lingering jet-lag, and end up in a grumpy mood that seriously clouds your judgement. Often a good night's rest can give you a whole new set of eyes on the world. If you arrive somewhere late at night, a place can seem like a horrible ghost town, but then you wake up to a wonderfully charming place that's buzzing with activity in the morning.

Sometimes you just get a sinking feeling that things aren't as fun right now as they were a while ago. If this happens, remember that travel is always full of such ups and downs. Maybe you just need to move on the next place and re-roll the dice.

If your trip lasts maybe a month or so, then you will be probably keen on maintaining momentum throughout. But if your trip is very open ended, you might well decide to linger somewhere for a while. Doing so can be a great way to connect with the culture, take time out to work, volunteer, take classes, or generally just to take a break from packing and unpacking every few days.

While sticking around somewhere for a while is nice, it's also very easy to get a little *too* comfortable and end up really being stuck. You might not even notice this at first, until one day you wake up suddenly realizing you've chewed all the flavour out of a place and urgently need to move on. Fortunately, it's easy to change your mind and shift gear very quickly.

For example, a couple of months into my first Southeast Asia trip I arrived on the Gili islands in Indonesia, thinking I would stay for only a few days before heading on to climb a nearby volcano. Instead I quickly realized that months of continuous nomadic life had left me utterly exhausted. And so I lingered on the island for weeks on end in what was mostly a sloth-like existence, and while I sometimes felt I was maybe missing out on other things, it also felt good to stay put for a while. That is, until I met a girl I really liked... who unfortunately already had to leave the island just two days later.

The morning after we'd said goodbye, I felt terrible. I sat on the beach, just staring at the horizon. Why wasn't I with her on Bali? We hadn't actually discussed such a plan, but it's where I really wanted to be.

I realized I'd made a huge mistake. I suddenly sprang into action and went through what seemed like a jump-cut montage from a movie: I grabbed all my stuff, chucked it into my bag, checked out, sent her a message that I was coming, quickly said goodbye to everyone in my hostel, and got on the first speedboat out of there. After weeks of inertia, it took just 15 minutes to kick myself back into gear. I didn't know if things would pan out, but I knew that in any case it was time to go. (It turned out to be a good decision, as we combined our travel plans and ended up travelling through all of Myanmar together. But even if that hadn't happened, I would have still been happy to be on the move again.)

Sometimes it isn't clear what you should be doing next, and sometimes it's completely obvious. If you don't know what to do, always go with your gut. Even when your gut *isn't* full of butterflies...

Dealing with travel fatigue

"Travel fatigue" is surely the epitome of a 1st world problem. (Oh poor you, so tired of travelling!) Still, travel fatigue is a real thing that many long-term travellers end up experiencing. It is unlikely to affect you if you're travelling for a number of weeks or months, but if your journey is many months, a year, or even longer, then you might just get stuck in a rut at one point.

Maybe you lose your enthusiasm for seeing yet another market, another church, or yet another waterfall. Maybe after all that freedom, you begin craving a clearer sense of purpose. Perhaps you get sick of other travellers coming and going, and regularly having to say goodbye to people heading off in other directions. Or maybe you just get a little homesick.

All this could be a sign that you need to start thinking about going home. Or maybe you just need a couple of days to recharge your batteries. Sometimes you might find that the adrenaline rush of arriving somewhere new can give you a big second wind.

Another good cure can be to take a vacation from your vacation, so to speak. Perhaps it's been a long time since you've last had that "Sunday afternoon in bed" feeling. So maybe book a nice room, have breakfast in bed, and just watch some movies all day. Other times a change of perspective is necessary: your interest in seeing just the 'sights' might begin to wane, but then you discover a whole new level to your journey by slowing down and really soaking in the cultures.

Travel ruts are inevitable if you're going to be on the road for a very long time. Travel can be like a party that never stops, so it's not that strange if you have a bit of a crash at some point. These feelings are often temporary, but if you find yourself stuck in a rut repeatedly, it might be time to (gasp!) reassess your journey...

Key points from this chapter

- Try to **balance planning ahead with improvising as you go**. A big trip can give you the freedom to follow your whims and discover things as you go. It is still worthwhile however to do at least some degree of prior research.
- **Expect your plans to change.** You can't exactly anticipate the weather, your mood, energy level, circumstances, and so on. Keep your plans flexible so that you can go with the flow.
- **You can't always be everywhere at the 'best' time.** Being somewhere in peak season has its disadvantages anyway. Don't feel bad about being somewhere in the shoulder seasons: it may in fact be unavoidable on a big multi-country trip. That said, you might still want to avoid the harshest months of the year (e.g. winter in Europe or monsoon season in Asia).
- Make sure you have **checked the visa requirements** for every country you intend to visit.
- **Travel guides paint rose-tinted pictures** but they can still be hugely valuable resources. They are especially great for general travel planning; online resources are often a little better for finding restaurants or hotels as they have more current information.

- **Use online resources** to help plan your trip and book accommodation while you are travelling. Some of the key websites are TripAdvisor, WikiVoyage, Hostelworld, and Agoda.

- There are many ways to **find places to stay.** You can opt to always pre-book them, or you can wing it and find something when you get there. Outside of important holidays or festivals (when things book out quickly), this is usually not a problem.

- You can **book tickets** for buses, trains, minivans, and so on at your place of accommodation, at the bus or train station, or at travel agencies. Booking them online is not usually so easy in developing countries, but in developed countries it can be faster than buying them in person.

- As an independent traveller you will often have to make **difficult decisions about where to go**, how long to stay somewhere, or what route to take. If you have researched the different options and still don't know what to do, try to just follow your heart. If a place ends up being disappointing, you can always move on.

[5]

Money-saving methods

IF YOU WANT TO TRAVEL for a long time, you might have to be a little more frugal. Fortunately, there are quite a few ways to keep your costs under control and make significant savings throughout your trip. Whether it is saving money on air fare, accommodation or food, being just a little bit savvy lets you travel longer for less.

Money-saving attitudes

First of all, you can make huge savings by shifting some of your attitudes. By sometimes going the extra mile (literally and figuratively), or having a willingness to adjust to the local lifestyle, you can end up spending far less money.

Vacationing versus travelling

When you're on a bigger trip, try not to spend like you're on a holiday. Your trip is going to be a marathon and not a sprint, after all. Think of yourself living nomadically rather than just being on a vacation, and let this inform the spending decisions you make. This doesn't mean you shouldn't splurge on worthwhile experiences from time to time, just that you may not need the ultimate in luxury or comfort constantly.

Going overland

Travelling overland is almost always cheaper than flying. A ten-hour bus journey is not as fast or as comfortable as a one-hour flight, but by trading in some convenience you will earn yourself some savings that will let you travel longer. Besides, you will see more of a country by traveling through it instead of flying over it. If you count the time spent at the airports, the time difference with overlanding is often not as dramatic anyway.

Adjusting to the local way of life

As they say, "When in Rome, do as the Romans do." If a country is famous for its wine, then drink wine instead of beer. It will cost less, and it will probably taste great. Conversely, a locally produced beer costs about half a dollar in Vietnam, while a glass of imported wine will cost you a small fortune there. Always adjust, at least for most of the time, to whatever is produced locally: eat rice in rice country, potatoes in potato country.

The same goes for your sleeping arrangements. For instance, in tropical countries, try to wean yourself off of air-conditioning and get used to sleeping in fan-only rooms. The locals can do without A.C. and so, probably, can you. If you give it some time, your body will adjust to the heat. Not booking A.C. rooms will shave off as much as 50% from your accommodation costs. (A good way to transition into this is to lower the setting of your A.C. by a few degrees every night until you no longer need it.)

Savings over convenience

It's easy to spend money out of pure convenience. For instance, many tourists will happily pay more for accommodation that is in an obvious central location, or for a place that can be more easily booked online. But if you have the time to research alternative hostels, or to stay a little further from where the action is, you will be travelling much more cheaply. If you're not in a hurry, you probably won't mind taking that 15 minute tuk-tuk ride into town if that means spending just half as much on your room.

Staying in hostels

Hostels are a great way to save money, though there are still often some misconceptions about them. While the old "youth hostels" of yore were rather grubby places that sometimes didn't even provide any sheets or bedding, modern hostels are typically very pleasant and comfortable places to stay, often offering dorms as well as private rooms, with proper showers and clean bed-sheets, free WiFi, and sometimes other amenities as well.

Even if you think you are not the type of person to stay in hostels, it's worth considering them for at least part of your accommodation needs, as they can really help keep costs down. Dorm beds are very cheap, especially if you are travelling alone and can't split the cost of a room among multiple people. When travelling as a couple or group, hostels can still be a great option particularly in capitals and larger cities where good budget-price accommodation can be more difficult to find. The free amenities at hostels can help you save money too; unlike hotels, they won't nickel-and-dime you for things like internet access. Above all, hostels are amazing places to meet like-minded people.

Since hostels are squarely targeted at backpackers—many of whom travelling long-term—much more effort is spent on creating a welcoming and communal atmosphere. Some hostels can even feel like a home away from home. Often there is an on-site kitchen, a common room where you can browse the internet or watch movies, or a bar area where you can grab a drink, chat with other guests, or play some cards. There is usually information about local activities, city maps, a book exchange, and other helpful services and resources.

Hostel dorm rooms come in all shapes and sizes. The most modern ones offer custom-built private sleeping cabins with all sorts of modern conveniences, while the most basic and lowest-priced ones might merely have some old creaky bunk beds. It depends a lot on where you are travelling (and how little you really wish to spend).

A $3 a night hostel in Laos might just provide you with only a mattress on the floor (which is common in many Asian homes) and a locker for your luggage, whereas a $30 a night hostel in London will get you a bed in a modern building with every possible bell and whistle included. (The clientèle will be different, too. In a cosmopolitan location like London you might find someone in full business attire practising for a job interview sitting right next to a dread-locked hitchhiker plucking their guitar. But in, say, rural Mexico, it's probably all going to be backpackers.)

Some travellers stay in hostels virtually all the time, while others just add it to the mix along with guesthouses, home-stays and budget hotels. Either way, hostels can be an excellent way to keep costs down.

Too old for hostels?

While hostels have, over the years, branched out to include a wider demographic (and are no longer typically referred to as "youth hostels"), they do still tend to attract a somewhat younger audience—often in their 20s to mid-30s. If you are a bit older, you might wonder if staying in hostels is still the way to go.

The truth is that it all depends. Firstly, it depends on what kind of hostel we are talking about. The majority of hostels are quite accommodating to all age groups, though some are still decidedly aimed at only the young and foolish. Checking hostel reviews in advance will easily tell you what kind of atmosphere to expect. For instance, if the description says "free beer on arrival", or if the hostel literally advertises itself as a party hostel, then the place is clearly going to be a lot younger and rowdier—and you should not go there expecting many deep conversations or, necessarily, a good night's rest.

It also depends on where exactly you are travelling. In easier and more mainstream destinations, the average age in hostels trends a little lower. Hostels in more 'serious' destinations (for lack of a less pretentious term) attract a broader age range overall.

For instance, hostels in Australia at times get flooded with wide-eyed 18 and 19 year olds on their first overseas trip, which could make an older traveller feel like they accidentally jumped into the kiddie pool, so to speak. But go to Malaysia, Myanmar, Guatamala or Colombia—just to name some countries that attract both novice and more experienced travellers—and you will find that hostels attract a broader crowd. Here the age barriers might just melt away, with 20-something students staying in the same hostels as the odd 60+ year old world-travelling vagabond, a̲n̲d̲ ̲.̲.̲.̲ thing in between.

If it's not age that concerns you but your increased expectations for privacy and comfort, then consider booking a private room in a hostel rather than staying in a dorm. If a hostel has a public bar, you could even stay in a nearby hotel but come around for socialising at the hostel in the evenings, essentially getting the best of both worlds.

Since the situation is a little different everywhere, you might just have to try out the hostel scene in a country and see if it suits your age or travel style.

Using the sharing economy

The internet has increasingly empowered private individuals to easily offer various services such as transportation, meals, and accommodation online. Making use of the so-called sharing economy can not only get you things cheaper, but they often also offer the chance of having increased contact with locals as well.

One of the best known sharing economy platforms is Airbnb (www.airbnb.com), which let you rent someone's apartment or room at prices well below that of hotels. Similar services include Wimdu, HomeAway, and Roomorama. The website Campinmygarden (campinmygarden.com) is like Airbnb but for... you guessed it, camping in people's garden.

A number of platforms exist allowing you to book a home cooked meal with locals, including Eatwith (www.eatwith.com), Kitchensurfing (www.kitchensurfing.com) and Colunching (www.colunching.com).

For ride sharing, the current big players are Uber (www.uber.com) and Lyft (www.lyft.com), whose apps let you get picked up by locals and dropped off where you need to be, at rates that are cheaper than official taxis.

Car sharing sites let you connect with people who have an empty seat available in their car. BlaBlaCar (www.blablacar.com) is big in Europe and Liftshare (www.liftshare.com) is big in the United Kingdom.

Hospitality exchange websites facilitate the sharing of a bed or couch for free. The biggest of these by far is Couchsurfing (www.couchsurfing.com), though you can also check out TrustRoots (www.trustroots.org) or Trampolinn (www.trampolinn.com). While these sites can get you free accommodation, this doesn't mean you have to be a cheapskate: it's nice to bring something to eat, drink or share with your host, and it's common to spend some time with your host unless there explicitly isn't such an expectation.

Another way to keep costs down, but which will be somewhat more involved, is to essentially work for your accommodation. Houseswapping or housesitting is a way of staying in someone's house for free, often for a couple of months, in exchange for looking after the house while its owners are away. Check out Trusted Housesitters (www.trustedhousesitters.com) or HouseCarers (www.housecarers.com). Farmstays let you sleep and eat for free on a farm in exchange for doing chores around the farm. The main platform for finding farmstays is WWOOF (www.wwoof.net). Another one is WorkAway (www.workaway.info).

While the sharing economy can be very helpful, you will find opportunities mostly in urban and well-connected places (apart from maybe WWOOF). While you will have no problem, say, finding Couchsurfing hosts in Berlin, you will struggle to find any in rural Bolivia, where no one would even think of providing a place to sleep without charging at least something. Use the sharing economy to keep costs down in more developed countries in particular.

Finding cheap flights

The cost of flights can make up a significant slice of your expenditures. Fortunately, you can make substantial savings by always digging around a bit to find the cheapest option.

The differences in ticket price can be so huge sometimes that the savings can easily represent weeks of additional travel. For instance, I was recently searching for flights from Miami International to Bogota in Colombia which were all in the €500 range, until I discovered flights leaving from nearby Fort Lauderdale airport costing as little as €120. That €380 saved is easily worth half a month of travel in Colombia.

There is unfortunately no silver bullet for finding cheap flights: often it just requires trying different search queries and seeing what comes up.

There are however some tips and tricks you can use to increase your chances of finding that amazing deal.

Finding cheap destinations to fly into

If you are not yet fully decided on where you are going, and you just want to know what countries or cities are cheap to fly into, a recommended tool to use is Kayak Explore (www.kayak.com/explore). Kayak is a good website to look for cheap flights generally, though it's their Explore feature that is really worth checking out. It lets you set your home airport and then presents you with a world map with the lowest prices for flights from your chosen starting point. This can help you find cheap destinations or cheaper airports to fly into that you may not have yet considered. Sometimes just starting your trip in a different country than you were originally planning (and finding onwards travel overland) can generate enormous savings.

Finding cheap long-distance flights

For long-distance and intercontinental flights, including the flight taking you to- and from home to your chosen part of the world, it is essential to use a dedicated flight search engine. Skyscanner (www.skyscanner.net) is a popular one that comes highly recommended. I personally love to use Momondo (www.momondo.com), as it has a few great features that help you dig deeper and find that hidden gem of a deal. Both these sites are independent aggregators combining the databases of many different booking sites, and so they give you more complete results than just one booking site will give on its own (e.g. Expedia or Trivago).

While using a flight search engine like Skyscanner or Momondo, you can use the following tips for finding the best flight options:

- If you are not married to any particular departure date, you can achieve some huge savings. Conduct some random experiments with your departure and return dates; add a few days here, subtract a few days there. Most search engines also let you tick a box indicating you are flexible on the dates. Keep playing with the dates until you're sick and tired of doing so. The search calendar is your friend; it's really worth just playing around with that for a while and seeing what happens.

- It's usually cheaper to fly earlier in the week than on weekends. When experimenting with different dates, try Mondays, Tuesdays or Wednesdays for best results.

- Include alternative nearby airports as this can sometimes save you money. Search engines can often automatically include nearby airports within a small radius (e.g. including all London airports) but you'll have to manually look for alternative airports that are a bit further away. There can be huge differences in price between airports in the same area, though there is also no golden rule here. Secondary airports are sometimes much cheaper as they charge less tax to the airlines for using them, so budget carriers often fly to these smaller airports. On the other hand, larger hub airports benefit from economies of scale and increased competition. Sometimes a smaller secondary airport also has a hidden cost if it is very far from the city, as you will be paying more for your ground transportation out of there.

- Consider alternate itinerary options entirely. As an example, if you're going to the southern coast of Thailand, instead of getting there from the capital Bangkok (which is the most obvious way) you could also get there from Singapore or from Kuala Lumpur in Malaysia (seems strange perhaps, but these airports are nearly equidistant to Bangkok). Have a look at your destination on a map to see what other options might be nearby; sometimes that better option might be just across a border.

- Time your booking well. According to research published by both Skyscanner and Momondo, the optimal timeframe to buy tickets is usually 5 to 6 weeks ahead of departure.

- Use Flight Insight on Momondo to get a big picture view of price factors on a particular route (this will answer questions like "what time of year is the cheapest?" or "when is the peak season?"). There is a video on my blog demonstrating how to use this feature.

Learn more about finding cheap tickets with my instructional video at:
http://www.indietraveller.co/articles/view/how-to-find-a-cheap-flight

Finding cheap short-haul flights

All of the previous tips apply to finding shorter regional or domestic flights as well. However, finding great deals for such shorter flights can require a bit more manual research as well. This is mainly because smaller budget- or domestic carriers are not always included in flight search engines or booking sites, which is particularly true for carriers in the less touristy parts of the world.

If you are looking for a flight from one remote place to another, it helps to look up their airports on Wikivoyage or on Google to find out which carriers go there. You can then check directly with these airlines. While it's still worth trying the search engines, it's often manual searches that get you the best options here.

For example, when I was travelling domestically in the Philippines, I found some great flights with local carriers Cebu Pacific and Zest Airways that were not listed on any search engine and were far cheaper. There is absolutely nothing wrong with such airlines; they just aren't hooked up to all the flight search systems, do not participate in online referral schemes, or focus mainly on domestic customers, and so they can be harder to find online. In my case, I had to type the name of a nearby small regional airport into Google, find out who actually flies there, and use the search functions of these airlines to compare prices.

Flying local

The more adventurous your location, the more adventurous your flights might become. One traveller told me the story of flying over the Amazon with a local carrier called Air Juan, tickets for which could only be purchased from an office somewhere in town. This ramshackle office did not have a printer, so the ticket confirmation consisted of a handwritten stub. The airplane turned out to be a small propeller plane. My friend got seated right behind the pilot, who was doing systems checks while pouring coffee from a thermos. Perhaps the pilot was, indeed, Mr. Juan himself.

Avoiding unnecessary fees

Before you book your flight, make sure you are not paying for extras you don't need. Check if your flight already includes baggage allowance. If it doesn't, you will have to pay extra. If it does, it may be set to 20kg by default when perhaps all you need is 10kg, so check if you can downgrade your allowance to save a bit of money. (Baggage fees are a good reason to pack light, as it lets you make due with just the cabin baggage allowance more often.)

Some low-budget carriers charge an extra fee for printing a boarding pass, which you can avoid by checking in online and printing it yourself, or showing a barcode on your smartphone if such a digital system is available. Some airlines let you exclude the in-flight meal from the price, which is great if it is a short flight and you don't mind bringing your own snacks. Finally, never tick the insurance box if you already have travel insurance yourself, as this will be redundant.

Saving money with reward programmes

Signing up to airline loyalty programs can be somewhat beneficial, as collecting enough airmiles (or similar reward points with other names) will let you book cheap reward flights. The flights you book with reward points are in theory free, but you still have to pay all the airport taxes, so this usually works out to about a third of the normal price.

Unfortunately, due to thinning margins in the airline industry, many reward programs have been completely hollowed out in recent years. The number of miles you need to fly before you can actually book a reward flight has increased dramatically across nearly all airlines. If you are a regular flyer, it can still make sense to collect points and to find out exactly how to maximize your rewards, but we're sadly no longer talking about the generous loyalty programs that travel hackers once obsessed over. Unless you are George Clooney in *Up In The Air*, it can take you a long while to get anything out of them.

If you do collect miles, try to collect them within same alliance as much as possible. That way you consolidate your points into one reward program. Some credit cards also let you save up airmiles with every purchase. If you use such a credit card regularly for a long time (e.g. at least a year) you can make some decent savings this way.

These days, if you have the choice between a more expensive flight that you can earn airmiles on with your loyalty card, or a cheaper flight with another carrier, the latter option is often the better one.

Spending the night in transit

When going overland you will often have the option of travelling at night. There are some good arguments in favour of doing so: you won't waste your day sitting in a bus doing nothing, and you avoid having to pay the cost of one night of accommodation.

On the other hand, while travelling at night can save you time and some money, it can be draining. If you are like me, you may struggle to get any decent sleep on a night bus. Even if you manage to sleep for a while, you may still be woken up every two hours or so during regular stops and toilet breaks. The time you think you are saving by travelling at night can easily be lost again in having to recover from lack of sleep after you arrive.

In Asia, night buses tend to be a lot of work, as they are usually very old buses that don't have on-board toilets, so they stop for toilet breaks constantly. Still, they can be hard to resist if you're on any kind of tight schedule, or simply eager to keep moving. In Europe and North America night buses are, unsurprisingly, a lot better. In South America the bus services are downright fantastic, especially if you get a fully reclining seat (tickets called "full cama"). What South America continent lacks in budget airlines it easily makes up for in affordable yet luxurious long-distance bus services.

Travelling by sleeper train is typically a lot more comfortable than a night bus (and there's a certain romance to travelling this way as well). Since you can lie down fully horizontally rather than sitting in a chair, you can usually get some decent shut-eye, and the rhythmic movements of the train may even cradle you to sleep. If you find that you can sleep well on trains, then the savings in time and money are almost definitely worth it.

When having to overnight somewhere between two different flights, some budget travellers will opt to spend that night at the airport instead of checking into a hotel for one night only. There is even a website dedicated to sleeping in airports, complete with tips and tricks on where to find a quiet spot to catch some Z's (aptly named www.sleepinginairports.net).

I did this once at Lima Airport, and to be honest, that night wasn't my favourite. My friend and I managed to find a spot in a relatively quiet corridor, though we were still constantly woken up by cleaning staff, people opening and shutting shops, and loud echoing announcements from the speakers. Since we couldn't find any chairs or benches, we were actually forced to sleep on the floor while resting our heads on our backpacks... and as it turns out floors at airports with AC become absolutely freezing after a while. Not awesome.

A year later I briefly considered spending the night at Jakarta International, but nightmarish post-traumatic flashbacks from Lima made me quickly abort that plan. I found a cab driver who knew a nearby budget hotel, and for $30 (including the ride) I got myself five glorious hours of sleep. I slept like a baby.

Sleeping at airports to save money isn't exactly a lot of fun (or maybe I am just not hardcore enough!), though it is often possible. The sleeping-in-airports website will tell you everything you need to know, and has a lot of information on lounges or budget hotels that are close to airports as well.

Saving money on cab fares

Cabs and other private transportation will often charge you way more than they should. When unmetered, it is not unheard for a cab driver to charge you up to five times the normal price. If you constantly let this happen, it can really add up over time.

Overcharging happens most easily when you have just arrived in a new place and you don't yet know the local currency or prices. Find out beforehand what a reasonable fare is by checking online or asking around, then let the cab driver know you are aware of the actual prices.

If during the ride the cab driver says something like "heeeey my friend, is this your first time in [name of whatever city you arrived]?", then you should go to yellow alert. While the driver may just be making some friendly chit chat, it is often a sign he is trying to figure out just how much you really know. Cab drivers prefer to use their tricks on tourists who are fresh off the boat, so to speak, as they are less likely to notice any overcharging and might not yet be familiar with the local prices or currency. Asking if it's your first time here is a way for them to assess the situation.

If the driver seems at all evasive about the price or the meter, or is just way too friendly to you and trying to distract you, go to red alert and scramble all jets... he is definitely going to overcharge you. Be clear and insist on the meter, or get out of the cab and find another one that will charge you an honest price.

Being firm but fair with drivers can save a lot of money. If someone is unwilling to drive you at a reasonable rate, there is almost always someone else who will.

Sometimes I like to pretend that I am an expat or have been to a city many times before, as this almost guarantees a fair price and avoids the driver taking the scenic route.

Saving money through haggling

Salespersons at markets, street stalls or in local shops will often quote you prices that are way higher than the actual fair price. However, in this case they are not necessarily trying to screw you over, but entirely expect you to make a counter proposal.

I didn't like haggling at first. I wished everyone just used sticker prices so that we wouldn't have to go through this silly bidding ritual, but I was forced to accept it as the way transactions work in some places. Now that I am used to haggling, I actually enjoy it.

Haggling is a bit like a game in which both parties know they are BS-ing each other a bit, but it's all in good fun. A salesman will surely not respect you for accepting the initial price, but a good haggle will result in a dignified transaction that leaves both parties happy.

Here's how it works. The salesman will first propose a price he knows to be extremely high. This is your cue to go into improvisational theatre mode: act like you are shocked, or act like you are sad that you cannot afford it. Say that you are sorry but that it is too much, or claim you or someone you know got the same item for much less somewhere else.

Now you should propose a price that you know to be way too low. It is the salesman's turn to put on his best acting face, as he will need to respond with incredulity. He will claim such a price would put him out of business... but then propose another price that is somewhere in the middle. Usually, this is the price that will still get him a very healthy margin, but is much fairer to you.

If you aren't hearing a better price, walk away. Pretend you are no longer interested while keeping a straight face. Move to the shop next door, or just turn around and walk away a few steps. Chances are the salesperson will ask you to come back, and will offer you a more reasonable price.

You can choose to stop haggling here—the salesman will be more than happy, and you are probably getting a good price. You could still try to nudge it down further, though the time to propose dramatically lower prices has passed; you should now be zeroing in on a compromise.

After this round, you will definitely have haggled enough, unless perhaps you are negotiating a very expensive purchase. While haggling is expected in many parts of the world it is rude to take it too far, as then you will just be a jerk trying to systematically reduce someone's profit margin.

There are a few additional techniques you can use to bargain down prices:

Technique 1: Pleasing the boss

This is a sort of Bad Cop, Good Cop scenario. In mid-negotiation, have your partner or travel buddy play the role of the unimpressed money manager advising you not to make the purchase. *You* would like to buy the item, but the boss is saying no. Salesmen will find this funny and are likely to lower the price.

Technique 2: Making them like you

Showing a salesman you have made the effort to learn a few local words, or that you are interested in their culture, will get you on their good side. They will stop seeing you as a typical tourist and will be more inclined to give you a good price. Approach the haggling as a social ritual.

Technique 3: The group haggle

If you are with a group, let one person do the talking. If you are not that person you have one task only: to stay in a holding pattern, ready to leave. For instance, if someone is negotiating the price of a tuk-tuk ride, don't undermine the process by already getting on board the vehicle... just loiter around for a minute while your friend does the talking. The designated negotiator may at some point pretend to be conferring with you about the price, in which case you should always just shake your head initially. If it's necessary to walk away from the deal, your task is to walk away as a group; the group haggle only works if you are in it together.

By the way, haggling does not typically apply to food or drinks or items with fixed prices. Don't try to talk down the price of your sandwich or that ticket for a regular scheduled bus, as you would no doubt get some serious blank stares.

Advanced low-balling

I used to ask cab or tuk-tuk drivers and market salesmen and the like how much something costs, but I realized later that this is clearly a rookie mistake. I mean, why would you ever do something as stupid as *ask for the price*? Presenting them with such an open question is just a big invitation for them to make something up on the spot. They'll often just tell you the highest price they think they can get away with, and from there it can take a long time to walk things back to a reasonable price. (We are talking here, of course, about any country where there is a big income disparity between locals and tourists.)

What I often do now, particularly with drivers, is to not even give them an opportunity to name their price at all. Instead I will flip the script and immediately suggest the lowest possible price that I can think of. Even when I don't know the actual price at all, I will just suggest one that's ex-

...ery low—really any price that seems just a hair short of being plain offensively low.

Saying "I need to get to the station. That's 10 Baht, right?" is much more likely to get you the actual local price of 30 Baht than saying "how much is it to the station?", as then negotiations will surely start at 150.

While this technique is very effective at getting you much more reasonable prices, it does still follow that good service should be rewarded. If someone is willing to charge you an honest price, you might want to also leave them a nice tip.

Booking online versus offline

You might think the best deals are always found online. For some things this is certainly true. If you're trying to buy some travel gear, it might be cheaper on Amazon or eBay than in a store. Looking for travel insurance? Then you should probably have a look at a price comparison website. And if you're looking to book a mid- or high-end hotel, Expedia probably has better rates for some hotels than if you were to book with those hotels directly.

But when it comes to less developed countries, and especially when it comes to booking tours and activities there, you will often find that the you can get the best deals in person.

In fact, some of the prices you find online for activities you can do in backpacking countries (such as guided treks, zip-lining, sailing trips, surfing lessons, and so on) are complete rip-offs. Often you will end up with the tour company that figured out how to be internet savvy and make a nice-looking website, and not necessarily the tour company that is actually the best or the cheapest. If they can get people to pull out their credit card while still at home, they can still charge multiple times of what it actually costs locally.

When you are there making a booking in person during your trip, and you're already accustomed to and aware of the local prices, you're in a much better position to get a fair price.

This also goes, to some extent, for accommodation. If you don't book online but just show up, you have the option of looking around and comparing different places, and maybe you find a gem of a hostel or hotel that isn't actually listed online.

Don't worry about this too much if going to a Western country as there the reverse is can be true, as online booking prices here are sometimes discounted. But if you're booking a particular experience in a developing country online, check thoroughly to make sure you are not overpaying.

Reducing banking fees

By far the best method of getting money out abroad is to use ATMs (also known as cashpoints), as they are widespread, convenient and can be trusted to use fair currency exchange rates.

Using an ATM abroad is not free however. Every time you get money out you will be charged a foreign transaction fee as well as a currency exchange fee. For instance, a bank might charge 2% for every overseas ATM transaction, along with a currency exchange fee on top. This can add up over time. Sometimes instead of a percentage there is fixed a minimum transaction fee, so getting smaller amounts out abroad becomes relatively more expensive.

Usually the best approach is to take cash out in larger volumes at a time from a reputable commercial bank ATM. If you can, avoid taking money out from smaller ATMs that you can sometimes find installed in convenience stores and other locations, as these tend to slap an additional fee on top of the regular transaction fee. Avoid making individual payments using a bank- or credit card as well, as these often come with additional fees (paying by card might not even be possible, as many local economies around the world are still very much reliant on cash transactions).

The cheapest and easiest way is almost always to get cash from a bank ATM and make any payments in cash. Use your bank debit card to withdraw cash and not a credit card (unless perhaps in emergencies) as this is significantly more expensive. A credit card company might charge, say, 12% for an ATM cash withdrawal while with a bank debit card this is typically in the 1-4% range.

Another method to reduce ATM fees is to open an account with a bank that doesn't charge any fees for foreign withdrawals. While large established banks rarely, if ever, offer this, some smaller independent banks do promote themselves by offering this feature.

Try to spend any leftover money before you leave, or just keep some of those bills as souvenirs.

In the United States, the Charles Schwab bank has a checking/debit account that doesn't charge ATM fees abroad, which has predictably become popular with long-term travellers and world nomads. In the United Kingdom, the little-known Metro Bank offers a similar deal. HSBC is another popular bank with world travellers—while they do charge ATM fees for withdrawals at other banks, they don't do so for withdrawals from their own ATMs, and HSBC is unusual for having branches all over the world.

Opening a new bank account just for your travels only makes sense, of course, if you are going away for a long enough time for these savings to be worthwhile. It's probably not worth bothering for a trip lasting a few months, but it may pay off very nicely if you are going away for, say, a year.

Another way of getting cash out abroad is with prepaid debit cards. You can load money onto them and then use these the same way as a regular bank debit card. The benefit of getting prepaid debit card(s) is mainly that you'll increase the number of ways you can get money out. Also, because they are not tied to your bank account, the amount that can be debited is capped, which makes it a little bit more secure.

When exchanging currencies, avoid doing so at airports as the rates there are often quite bad. If you have a smartphone, download a currency conversion app to help you check if an exchange rate is fair.

Whenever you enter a new country, it's a good idea to immediately familiarize yourself with the new currency. I usually write down the exchange rate and a few conversions on a piece of paper as a cheat-sheet which will get me through the first few days. It also helps to memorize the colours and shapes of the bills—some currencies are not very well designed and have two bills with very similar colours, which can lead to mistakes.

Before you leave a country, try to convert any cash you have left and spend your loose change. Some currencies are considered very obscure in international markets and cannot be easily exchanged outside of their country of origin (for instance Vietnamese Dong or Bolivian Bolivianos).

Dealing with fussy ATMs

Getting money out from ATMs is usually easy and convenient. But from time to time, an ATM might give you some trouble.

Don't be surprised if you get an error message that doesn't make sense. Sometimes it will say "wrong number" (presumably referring to PIN) when you *definitely* typed in the right PIN. Occasionally it will say you have exceeded your overdraft limit even when there's still plenty of funds left in your account. Sometimes an ATM will simply tell you a transaction cannot be authorized and just spit your card back out.

We're not talking about sketchy ATMs here, but ones from reputable banks that still occasionally act up. 95% of the time you can get money out just fine, but if you get an unusual error message, don't panic immediately. Try a few other ATMs first, or try the same ATM the next day (when it might have been restocked with new money). If problems persist, you may want to try calling your bank to see if any anti-fraud measures may have been triggered, as sometimes this happens by mistake.

Miscellaneous money saving tips

Here are a few more quick tips on how you can save money on your trip:

- Avoid eating Western style food all the time and try the cheaper local fare.
- Eat away from the tourist hotspots where the food is much more expensive.
- Drink local alcoholic drinks instead of imported brands. Adjust to whatever is produced in the country you are in.
- You can use Skype (or similar) to call regular phone numbers. This is much cheaper than using a phone to make international calls, as Skype will charge you only at the local rate for the country you are calling. Keep some credit in your Skype account for when you need to call home or check your voicemail.
- Buy a local SIM for your mobile phone to reduce any call or data fees. Some Android phones even let you store two SIMs, so that you can switch between your home number and your temporary local number on the fly.
- Bring an ISIC student card if you are a student. You can get this at www.isic.org and it can often get you all sorts of discounts.
- Stay in towns or the countryside more than in cities. Major cities are always more expensive.
- Resist buying trinkets everywhere. People will try to sell you souvenirs constantly, but try to limit yourself to buying only a couple of souvenirs that you really like.
- If you are travelling in country where inexpensive food is not so widely available, stay in a hostel with kitchen facilities and cook your own food.
- Prices are lower when travelling out of season.
- Knowledge is power. Always be curious and ask people you meet where they booked things and how much they paid for it.

Thinking in averages

While you should keep an eye on your spending, make sure you also take the long view; don't worry *too* much about temporary spikes in costs.

Prices can fluctuate a lot as you travel. One day you may be in a touristy location where something costs $10, the next day you may be in a remote little village where that exact same thing costs just $2. Whole countries can vary in cost depending on the strength of their currency, their overall wealth, and even their taxation regimes (e.g. alcohol can be dirt cheap in some countries and taxed heavily in others). Sometimes you will be on a two-hour flight that costs as much as your last ten bus journeys, or having a Western-style meal that costs as much as five local meals.

Focusing on this too much can drive you crazy, which is why it helps to think in averages. You will feel better about spending a little more sometimes if you remember that you are still not spending a lot overall. It can be tempting to compare apples to oranges, even complain about the absurdity of price differences, but this is just how things are. As long as you remain reasonably disciplined with your spending, things will probably still balance out in the end.

Even on a backpacker budget, it's okay to spend a little more from time to time. Eating local food is by far the cheapest, but every now and then you might just crave some Western food. The pizza costing three times as much as the local meal can seem like an extravagant indulgence, but a few local meals later and much of that cost has flattened out. Similarly, for every night you stay in a dirt cheap hostel, you can see yourself collecting imaginary coupons towards the next time you want to stay in a nice hotel.

It's not so much about how much you are spending in a given day, but how much you are spending on a weekly or monthly basis; inevitably you will have your share of expensive and inexpensive days.

The Angel's Share

There is a concept in whiskey and wine-making called the Angels' Share. A percentage of all the raw stuff they put in a barrel for ageing actually evaporates over the years, which is said to go to the 'angels'. For example, about 10% of a barrel of whiskey disappears into thin air before it has finished maturing, and there's nothing even the most skilled distiller can do to stop this. It's simply the cost of making a great whiskey.

Similarly, the cost of going on a great journey is that you will inevitably lose some money along the way. Expect that at least some small part of your budget will evaporate due to dumb or unforeseen things. It's the Angel's Share of travel.

Maybe you find out, just after booking, that you could have gotten the same ticket cheaper somewhere else. Maybe you forget your phone charger and now need to buy a new one. Maybe someone rips you off and you end up spending more on a ride than you should have. This sort of thing happens all the time.

As much as you might wish to be amazingly frugal and efficient all the time, your spending will never be completely perfect. There are always some inefficiencies.

Learn from mistakes, but don't beat yourself up too much either. You can try to keep your money away from those angels' greedy hands, but they always find a way to impose their tax. Manage your spending as well as you can, but know that in the end you can't always optimize everything.

Key points from this chapter

- Saving money starts with having the right attitude. Don't **spend as though you are on holiday**, try **travelling overland** as much as possible, and **adjust to the local ways**.
- **Hostels** can help you keep costs down, are great places to meet other travellers, and have all sorts of services and facilities that make your life on the road a little easier.
- The **sharing economy** can get you a lot of things free or cheaper than usual (though these platforms are most effective when travelling in urban or well-connected destinations).
- You can use a variety of techniques to **find cheap flights**.
- Sometimes you can save money by **spending the night in transit**, for instance by taking a night bus or night train, or sleeping at an airport. Weigh the pros and cons of doing so.

- You can **save money on cab fares** by avoiding any overcharging and by always insisting on using the meter.
- You can **save money through haggling**, a somewhat theatrical negotiation process that you sometimes need to go through when purchasing at a market, or when agreeing on a price in advance for, say, a tuk-tuk or boat ride.
- **Booking things offline** is often cheaper when travelling in the developing world.
- You can **reduce banking fees** by using your debit card only. For very big trips, it's worth setting up a bank account that you can make international withdrawals from for free.
- A frugal attitude should not get in the way of your trip enjoyment. It's a good idea to **think in terms of averages** rather than agonising over every little cent that you spend.

[6]

How to pack and travel light

INEXPERIENCED TRAVELLERS tend to overpack. They often travel with big bulking backpacks designed not for travelling but for long-distance trekking. They fill these to the brim with an outsize wardrobe, too many pairs of shoes, unnecessary equipment and a plethora of travel gadgets brought just-in-case but most of which end up never leaving that bag at all. They sweat, they toil, they curse.

This is not a great way to travel. The more items you bring, the more you will burden yourself with carrying, storing, and looking after those items all the time. Packing less is better. After all, you want to feel free like a bird, not packed like a mule.

It's easy to see where to instinct to overpack comes from: usually it's what we already know from going on holidays. The process for packing for a shorter holiday is typically not so complicated, especially if that holiday is going to be in a fixed location: you just grab a big suitcase and fill it with whatever you think you'll need. For clothing, you might just grab multiples of everything so that you can simply choose what to wear at your destination. Carrying a heavy suitcase is, after all, not that big of a deal if you're only going to be in transit for a short period of time or visiting only a few places.

For long-term travel, a more considered approach is needed. Being light on your feet has many advantages, especially when you won't just be rolling luggage trolleys around at airports or taking taxis everywhere. Imagine running with all your luggage to catch a last train, wading through shallow waters to board a catamaran, or trying to cram your bag into the luggage rack of a rickety local bus that's already stuffed with bags of produce and live chickens. Big luggage is just awkward in these situations.

Clearly, backpacking demands a bit more mobility than conventional travel. But even the less adventurous long-term traveller will still be faced with having to pack and carry their luggage again and again. Keeping things lean will save yourself a lot of sweat and tears.

It seems that, inevitably, every traveller learns the value of packing light eventually. I once had to help carry people's bags onto a boat in Panama when one nearly did my back in, surely weighing at least 30 kilograms. It required two people to get the bag on board, hoisting it up as though it was a bodybag containing some monstrous cadaver. This bag's owner confessed that it had been doing her back in for weeks, and swore she would never pack so much again. On Bali in Indonesia I met a guy so frustrated with carrying too much stuff around that he donated half his clothes to a local charity. Before he had arrived at this decision, he told me he despised his heavy bag so much he wanted to burn it in a fire.

This is why, for a big trip at least, it is better to err on the side of packing less and not packing more. Try to get into the mind-set that everything you bring has a hidden cost: that of you having to physically take it everywhere.

Another aspect worth examining is the bag itself. You may of course already have a backpack that you can use, though perhaps you will want to buy a backpack specifically for your trip. If you have some money to spend, investing in a good backpack will pay off generously in terms of comfort and convenience.

Backpacks, by the way, offer many advantages over suitcases—at least for the type of travel covered in this book. Travelling with a suitcase is not ideal unless you plan to spend time exclusively in comfortable tourist hotspots or in modern and easy-to-navigate cities. Hard-shell suitcases are particularly cumbersome, and wheeled luggage is especially awkward when walking along dirt roads, cobblestone streets or sandy beaches.

Travellers keep telling me that, in hindsight, they feel they spent too much time prior to their trip trying to plan out their itinerary in too much detail, while not spending enough time packing well. Travel plans can remain quite fluid, and figuring out the precise details of your trip is arguably better done on the ground than at home. The opposite is true for getting your luggage and its contents right: this is far easier done before than during your trip. Properly taking care of this now will pay dividends throughout your journey.

The case for a smaller backpack

The iconic image of the backpacker is that of someone with a bulging 70+ litre bag on their back, so huge that it towers above their head. While there isn't necessarily anything wrong with using such bags, they are not always the best option, and they are certainly not a requirement for being a "true traveller".

If you are planning to go wilderness hiking you may well need such a large backpack, as you will need the extra space to store a sleeping bag, tent, tarp, and all sorts of other camping gear. But if you are planning to sleep in hostels, guesthouses or hotels, you will almost certainly be fine with something a little smaller.

Before my first backpacking trip, someone recommended I get the biggest bag possible because "you never know when you'll need that extra space". So I bought a 70 litre bag with a 15 litre day-pack expansion. After a quick packing test, I realized I shouldn't have heeded this advice. The metal frame alone weighed several kilos, and after a realistic assessment I decided it was complete overkill for my needs. I went back to the store and exchanged it for a smaller 40 litre bag. I'm very happy I did.

Many world travellers recommend 40 or 50 litre bags as they make for quite a wonderful 'just right' size. Luggage size is typically expressed in litres of volume which may not be the most intuitive measure, but imagine a 40 litre bag sitting somewhere between the really big trekking backpacks and smaller 20-25 litre daypacks or school backpacks.

On the left is a 70+10 liter backpack, on the right a 40 liter backpack.

Other travellers are sometimes surprised to see my modestly sized backpack. "You're travelling the world with *that*?", they ask as they nearly collapse under the sheer weight of all the stuff they're carrying on their backs. Their surprise quickly turns into envy.

The strange thing about using a large backpack, like those 60, 70 or even 90 litre ones, is that you will inevitably find a way to fill it completely. Much like air sucking into a vacuum, the availability of space can somehow compel you to use it. A smaller bag forces you to be smarter and more disciplined.

A smaller and lighter bag is also much easier to handle during transit. You can easily swing it onto the back of a tuk-tuk or tricycle. You can tuck it under your seat in a bus, where it is more secure while also easier to access than a bag kept in the cargo hold. And if you pack very light, you may not even have to check in any luggage at airports, saving you money on baggage allowance.

There are many other advantages. A smaller and lighter bag makes you stick out less in a crowd, and it is easier to keep your belongings organized when you are carrying less stuff. It will, of course, also be easier to walk around with. When you arrive in a new place you won't be compelled to just take the first (and not necessarily best) accommodation available, because you can walk around more easily to find that place you really want to stay.

A bag with a capacity of around 40 litres isn't exactly small but it is a lot smaller than most. When my 40 litre bag is filled with clothes, toiletries, laptop, book and shoes it weighs about 12 kilos (26 pounds). This is light enough to carry in reasonable comfort when looking for accommodation or when in transit.

While much less common, I have seen people travel even lighter. A friend travelled through Europe with just a 25 litre bag, which is just the size of a school backpack. Perhaps this will give you a very high level of freedom and mobility, but to achieve this level of minimalism you will need to be truly ruthless in your packing decisions. If you are using such a small bag on a longer trip you are potentially wading into "reusing underwear" territory, so this is not generally recommended unless you are really trying to make a point. A bag can be too small. A mid-size is ideal.

Travelling with two bags

It's worth considering having two bags: your main mothership bag that contains most if not nearly all of your stuff, along with a much smaller daypack detachment that you can use during hikes, day-trips, or when exploring a city. Having a secondary bag can give you a bit more versatility, as it lets you store one bag in a cargo hold or locker while keeping the other one closer with you. A daypack can also provide quick access to a book, snacks, or a rain poncho while you are out and about.

Some backpacks come with integrated detachable daypacks. There are also lightweight mini daypacks that can be folded up and stored when you're not using them. You could also simply get a small (e.g. 10-15 litre) secondary backpack. You can carry this on your chest while your main bag is on your back (the "turtle shell" method of carrying two bags) or you can carry the daypack alongside you as though it is a briefcase. That probably sounds awkward, and it is a little bit, but it's worth it just for having a small bag for your more everyday use.

Finding the right backpack

It can be difficult to decide on the right backpack to purchase as there are countless models and manufacturers. It's not so useful to list specific products here as there is a huge number of brands with varying availability in each market. It is however possible to give some general tips that can help you make the right decision for you.

Firstly, consider exactly how you will be taking your belongings in and out of the bag, especially if it is top-loading. It's frustrating to have to take everything out just to get something from the bottom. This is where it helps to have separate compartments, or a duffel-style design that can zip open along the vertical axis.

Try out some different bags in a store instead of buying something online as this will give you some first-hand impressions. See how the backpacks feel on your back, and check if they have comfortable padding on the back as well as around the straps.

Many backpacks have back padding designed to maintain some airflow. This can be especially helpful if you are going to a warm climate or travelling during summer.

Check if the zippers have rings on them for attaching a padlock or wire lock. This won't stop a determined thief but does add an extra layer of security by preventing quick access to the most important contents of your bag.

A hidden compartment is another useful security feature. Some backpacks have, for instance, a tiny secret zipper with just enough space to store a passport and some money. This can make you feel assured that if someone were to quickly raze through your bag, they wouldn't find your most important items.

Since many people travel with electronics, a lot of bags also feature a padded laptop compartment. This can keep your laptop or tablet safe and is also a great place to store your travel documents.

Make sure the bag is made of water-resistant material or that it has a rain cover. Check the stitching and seams to judge the quality even if you are dealing with a trusted brand. The most vulnerable element seems to be where the shoulder straps are attached, so check this carefully. (I have personally had two cheaper bags break here).

Take the bag home, leave the tags on, and try to fill it with your essential items. Imagine using and carrying this for the next however many months you are travelling. If it doesn't feel right for your purposes, you can still exchange it for a more suitable one.

When it comes to your bag, quality does matter. To give a personal example, I bought a somewhat more expensive but higher quality bag which has held out perfectly fine. I also twice bought a cheap daypack on sale and these practically disintegrated after a few weeks. What seems like a good deal can actually be a waste of money, as not all backpacks are designed with the rigours of extended travel in mind.

There is a time for being frugal, which is on your trip itself, but when it comes to your bag it's not a bad idea to make a minor investment. Something in the €100 to €200 range will usually get you something good. Keep in mind that this bag is going to hold all your belongings, including valuables or electronics. It has to keep everything secure when being handled by airport, train or bus staff, has to stay dry when it's raining, and has to not rip at the seams. Most importantly, it has to be comfortable for you to wear. Since your bag has so many important tasks to fulfil, it seems that a little extra investment can go a long way here. Remember that a good backpack might last you ten years or longer.

The 100% essential items to bring

Assuming you have found the right backpack for your trip, you will now need to start assembling and packing your gear. Since we are focused on minimalism, let's start with the very basics first.

There are actually only a handful of items that are absolutely essential and that could ruin your trip if you happened to forget them. Access to money and your ability to cross borders are paramount, therefore the absolute key items not to ever forget are:

- **Your ID(s)** (passport, driving license, ID card)
- **Any country visas you may have arranged in advance**

- **Bank or credit cards**
- **Any PIN device needed to access your internet banking** (if applicable)

Since these items are so essential, be sure to store them securely. If you have multiple bank or credit cards, split them across multiple pockets or hiding places. If you are travelling with a partner, carry different bank cards in both your bags in case one person's card(s) will get lost or stolen.

For additional back-up, bring some emergency cash that you can use in a pinch (for instance if ATMs are being uncooperative). US dollars are preferable as they are accepted or exchanged virtually anywhere. Around $50 to $100 is a good amount to have as a cash reserve per person.

It's also a good idea to make some photocopies of your passport. A photocopy will obviously not pass for a real ID, but it can offer some basic identification if needed. For instance, you may wish to keep a copy with you while out and about, while keeping your actual passport in a secure locker or safe at your place of accommodation. Tour agencies or rental companies will sometimes ask for a copy of your passport as well.

If the worst comes to pass and you were to lose your passport or your ability to get money, this doesn't mean your situation is completely hopeless just yet. Passports can be replaced abroad at an embassy or consulate of your country, though this is usually for a hefty fee and can take considerable time. If you lose your bank card, your bank may be able to send a replacement to your current location by post if they are a particularly helpful bank. If they can't arrange this for you, you can still rely on sending money to yourself (or having someone from your family do this back home) via a Western Union branch or an online money sending service such as Azimo.com. However, this is much more cumbersome than simply walking to an ATM and so this is a situation you will definitely want to avoid.

While you can still survive in the worst case scenario, clearly you will want to look after your identification and your bank card(s) carefully. Try to keep them in the same secure place consistently.

The pitfalls of packing lists

Now that we have talked about the utmost essential items to pack, let's start tackling the entire category of "everything else".

When it comes to deciding what to bring along on your journey, it is easy to fall into the trap of bringing too much. Once you begin telling yourself that you should pack something "just in case", you are already on a slippery slope to overpacking.

Unfortunately, some of the packing lists available on the internet only add confusion. Seemingly every travel blog out there offers their own packing list, each offering different recommendations. Some packing lists are absurdly long, featuring over a hundred items. Some are focused purely on city travel, while others deal with backpacking in developing countries. Some lists are made for travelling through multiple climates, others for just one. Keep in mind that what may be right for one person may not be right for you and your specific trip.

What makes packing lists even more problematic is the term "backpacking", which can be used to mean both independent travel and wilderness hiking. Many packing lists are intended for campers and trekkers, but are easily mistaken for travel packing lists. As a result, many non-essential items make it into traveller's backpacks even though they are recommended only for those wanting to hike the wilderness with their own camping gear, food supplies, and so on—which is a whole different ball game.

For example, if you're out camping in a forest without access to drinking water then having a water-purifying system is unquestionably useful, but if you're travelling and staying in hostels, hotels or guesthouses, you will virtually always have safe drinking water nearby... and that water-purifying system will never end up being used.

This book is not about self-sufficient trekking or mountaineering; it assumes you will typically seek a local guide or touring agency if you want to go on such adventures during your trip. If you do wish to climb mountains on your own, hike independently, or camp in the wild, it is essential to seek extensive advice specific to these activities. It can be potentially dangerous if you don't know what you're doing, and especially if you're going to do this in difficult countries where paths aren't marked, maps are poor, and conditions are tough. (Some countries are blessed with national parks with amazing facilities and clearly marked trails, but internationally this is much more the exception than the rule.)

For the average traveller going far abroad, it's better to pursue adventure activities as part of an organized tour using professional guides. Not only does this ensure a higher level of safety, but any necessary equipment will already be provided for you. For instance, if you want to do a multi-day hike to the fabled Inca ruins of Machu Picchu, there is a plethora of reputable local guides and trekking companies that can take you there—they can even set you up with tents, food supplies, porters, and so on.

This is basically a long way of saying that tents, camping equipment, or hiking-, sports- and survival gear are not necessary unless you are certain you are going to use them regularly. So simply forget about the camping stuff if you are going to be constantly sleeping under a roof. As for the sports and adventure gear: typically, so long as you have some good walking shoes (more on this later) and some clothes that can get dirty, you are all set for doing adventure activities during your trip. This can take a lot of weight off your shoulders—literally.

So if you do read packing lists, make sure they apply to your style of travel. A final thing to keep in mind is that packing lists sometimes try to be too original by including weird and unusual travel gadgets as supposedly 'must have' items on their list. Always apply a pinch of scepticism, as anything that seems too clever for its own good probably is. A solar calculator? Not needed. An inflatable coat hanger for drying your clothes on? Nah, probably not. (Yes, that is a real thing.) The more unusually specific a travel gadget, the less likely it will serve you well on a day-to-day basis.

You can always buy it there

Do you live in fear of forgetting to pack something? Don't let the thought stress you out too much. If you do at least a decent job of packing and, of course, remember to bring the absolute essentials (passport, money, and so on) then you can always correct any minor oversight. Perhaps you do forget to pack, say, that nail clipper you desperately need, but this is clearly not the end of the world. Little things like this can always be purchased at your destination if and when you need them, which is especially true when travelling in developing countries where many things are very cheap to buy or replace. This is not trying to advocate wasting money on things you could have just packed back home: the point really is not to let a nail clipper keep you up at night. Do the best job you can given what you know now.

Packing your clothes

Could you imagine wearing the same shirt or top twice in a row at school or at work? Oh, the horror! Everyone would surely be wondering what you were up to last night! This just goes so show that we (understandably) care a lot about what we wear, and we equally care about what other people think about what we wear.

At home you have the luxury of a full wardrobe with many combinations of clothing that you can cycle through over the course of many weeks or even months. When you are packing clothes for your travels you are likely still in the mind-set you have at home, making it very easy to pack too much. Even if you think you are packing modestly, you are probably still taking way more clothes than you really need.

Chances are that when you are travelling you won't quite care as much about having a huge wardrobe, nor will other people be overly concerned with whether you've dressed to impress. You can get by with less, while still being comfortable and having something nice to wear every day.

You typically don't need to pack more than about a week's worth of clothing. Despite what some sources claim, dealing with laundry while travelling is fairly easy—meaning it's not an issue to cycle continuously through a more limited set of clothes.

Hostels in Western countries often have a washing machine that you can use, or their staff can point you to nearby coin-up washing machines. Some travellers use a universal plug stopper and some hand-wash soap so they can do their own laundry using any sink.

Laundry service is generally very cheap in developing regions such as in Asia or Latin America, sometimes costing as little as a dollar per kilo. Many hostels or guesthouses will happily take your dirty laundry at reception and will get it back to you clean the next day. If you are okay with dealing with laundry occasionally, then you won't need to pack many weeks worth of clothes.

Try to plan your travel wardrobe in a way that everything fits with everything else. That way you can always put something nice together even as your options decrease as you approach laundry day.

Avoid non-versatile clothing items, such as a dress or a shirt you would only wear on specific occasions. Avoid high-maintenance clothing as well, i.e. anything with non-standard washing instructions. Finally, go easy on packing white clothes as these tend not to stay white for very long (due to active or outdoors situations, or laundry services that can't always be relied on for washing these separately). It's not a hard-and-fast rule that you shouldn't bring any whites, though darker shades or colours are definitely much less delicate.

If you plan to travel through multiple climates, consider buying some clothes locally at the time that you need them. You could spend a lot of time in a warm climate, then buy some long trousers and sweaters only when you transition into a colder climate.

For instance, many travellers following the Latin American "Gringo Trail" will happily travel with just a basic selection of summer clothes, then buy some warm alpaca wool clothing only once they hit the colder Andes mountain range in Peru, Bolivia or Chile (a nice sweater made from alpaca wool costs about $8 in Bolivia).

Clothes are typically inexpensive in developing countries, so you may wish to keep some space in your bag for extra clothes you pick up along the way.

When packing for cold weather, the adage "don't pack wool, pack layers" is a good one to follow. Instead of wearing just one extremely thick wool jumper, you will benefit more from layering—for instance, having a sweater on top of a long-sleeve and t-shirt with a lightweight wind breaker on top.

Using individual layers instead of one wool layer keeps you warm while giving you more flexibility.

Choose versatile clothes

Ideally, most of your items of clothing should go happily together with most other items. Avoid packing, say, something in a crazy colour that only looks good when worn as part of a particular outfit. Choose clothes that you are comfortable with, that you can wear the majority of the time, and that combine easily. This ensures you will maximize the number of variations within your smaller travel wardrobe, and that you will always have some good options available.

Jeans or no jeans?

Some travel gurus advise against bringing denim jeans. They are bulky and slow to dry, the theory goes, so you should bring only lightweight quick-drying travel trousers. Personally, I see the point but am not entirely convinced, as there are still some good arguments in favour of bringing jeans. If you really enjoy wearing jeans, you might as well bring a pair.

While it's true that lightweight trousers somewhat reduce your packing weight and volume, the weight difference is fairly minor. And then there are times when it's just nice to have some jeans; in particular, they allow you to blend in and look less like a tourist when needed.

In temperate climates, it's easy to wear jeans often (or even all the time, depending on the season). However, rain can quickly make jeans smell like wet dog, and your travel schedule may not let you dry or wash them immediately, so a rain poncho that covers your legs can be very useful to have.

Jeans are admittedly much less useful in hot climates nearer the equator, though there are still occasions here where you may be glad to have them with. For instance, you might be in a more urban environment where shorts are less commonly worn, or you could end up spending time with locals or expats instead of other travellers, in which case the dress code might be a bit different. For example, one time I met up with an expat friend in Singapore and he took me out to some upmarket cocktail bars, which was a fun change of scene after spending months in funky backpacker hostels. It was nice to have jeans to wear and not, say, convertible zip-off khaki hiking trousers.

That said, if you are going to a hot climate you will definitely be wearing shorts, a sarong or skirt the vast majority of the time (think 95%+). Long trousers (jeans or otherwise) are just too uncomfortable in the heat. That pair of trousers will undoubtedly sit in your bag unused for ages, but every now and then may come a rare situation in which they come in handy—typically either when you are in a city or when you are in a colder high altitude area.

Then again, zip-off trousers with lots of cargo pockets are much more versatile for adventure travel purposes and do dry faster as well. Consider the climate and type of activities you expect to do, and go with whatever trousers seem most appropriate. Pack jeans if you think you will wear them.

Footwear

It seems there are as many opinions about travel footwear as there are travellers. Everyone swears by a different type of footwear, and travel forums are constantly ablaze with somewhat pointless debates on the subject (like which brand makes the better travel sandals—Teva or Chaco).

While there isn't a "best" type of footwear for travel—because it all depends on what you find most comfortable—it is fair to say that some types of shoes or sandals are more suitable than others. Let's walk through some of them.

High-top hiking or mountaineering boots

Are you planning to hike the Himalayas for several weeks? Then these are a worthy investment. But boots are not that versatile for more general travel use, and will take up a lot of space. As these shoes are rather specialized while very bulky at the same time, they don't make for the most practical type of footwear for long-term travel.

Low-top walking shoes

A simple pair of low-cut walking shoes can be used in many scenarios, including trekking, walking around towns or cities, and other everyday use, making it a great option for travel. Look for soles with good grip. A water-resistant and breathable mesh is another helpful feature. Walking shoes can be your all terrain workhorse; a recommended option.

Running shoes

A decent option, but not ideal. Running shoes can be comfortable, though they are ultimately designed for running and not for walking. One potential issue with running shoes from sports brands (especially ones like ASICS and Adidas) is that this might achieve a look that's strongly associated with a certain type of American tourist. If you wish to blend in and attract less attention from touts and the like, leave the running shoes (and the fanny packs) at home.

Sneakers

Sneakers are not necessarily the most versatile, though they do have some advantages. Low-top canvas plimsolls (such as those by Converse) are easy to fold up and tuck into a backpack. They can be a decent option, so long as you are not planning on doing anything *too* crazy with them, as their soles are not ideal for most outdoors activities. Sneakers are generally quite suitable for city activities or even for going out however, and they can make for a decent general back-up option for footwear.

A similar case can be made for desert boots made of suede or soft leather: because of their flexible material they are easy to compress and store in your luggage, and while their soles tend to be quite flat and not really suitable for all terrain, they can be of good use in cities in particular.

Flip-flops (a.k.a. thongs, slippers or jandals)

Flip-flops are the staple footwear for backpacking in warmer climates, and you may be surprised by how quickly you can adjust to wearing these nearly all the time. Many a traveller ends up wearing flip-flops extensively, though not everyone takes a liking to them equally.

It's key to find a size that's just right for you: if a pair of flip-flops is too loose-fitting, you may try to hold onto it with your toes with each step you take, which is a very uncomfortable way to walk. If it's too tight, the strap can seriously chafe your skin. Look for flip-flops that allow a slight gap between your foot and the strap, but not so much that you need to spend effort to keep them from slipping off your feet.

One neat advantage of flip-flops is that they can be incredibly inexpensive. You can pick up a half-decent pair for under $5 in many Asian or Latin American countries (nothing fancy, just regular foam soles and fabric straps). Walking on these continuously will probably wear them out in a month or two, though they are easy to replace.

In many cultures it's customary to take off your shoes before entering a shop or a home, and this is easiest when wearing some sort of flip-flops.

Sandals

Sandals range from the highly fashionable to the purely practical. For travel, many swear by sandals by brands such as Teva, Chaco or Taos, which are often water resistant and have good soles suitable for walking on multiple surfaces.

Sandals can be a little bit of everything. Like flip-flops, they let your feet breathe easily. Like shoes, many sandals offer good arch support. And some types of sandals, much like hiking shoes, have ribbed soles and other such features making them very useful for outdoor activities.

It's no wonder that so many travellers swear by sandals: they are clearly the most versatile footwear you can buy.

Flats

Women also have the wonderful option of wearing flats, which take up nearly no weight or space. They may not be appropriate footwear for all uses, but since they are so light you can't go wrong with throwing a pair into your backpack.

Barefoot

Sometimes the best footwear is no footwear. Have you found your perfect deserted island? Then why not become one with nature.

So... what footwear is best?

The answer to this question ultimately depends on what type of weather you think you'll have to deal with, as well as what you are generally most comfortable with. By applying common sense and considering the local climate and time of year, it's not too difficult to make the right choices. Breathable or open footwear is clearly preferable for hot and humid places, while something a little more closed and sturdy works well for colder places.

Try to pick two pairs of footwear or maybe three at most, and try to cover different common use scenarios for travel. This means you can probably leave high heels at home. If you can, avoid high top shoes or bulky boots that take up a lot of space needlessly.

I personally travel with flip-flops (wherever these are practical) combined with a pair of good low cut walking shoes. In destinations where the weather is colder, I might go for a pair of walking shoes and a pair of canvas sneakers. However, such preferences are quite personal, and you shouldn't let anyone else decide this for you. For example, I have a purely irrational fashion aversion to sandals which has kept me travelling with flip-flops even after two years on the road, despite knowing that sandals are a lot more comfortable overall. This probably makes me a grudging advocate of sandals, even though I shouldn't be.

One thing to keep in mind is that footwear is not always easy to buy locally if you need a larger size, as people aren't very tall on average in some countries. It's best not to accidentally leave your shoes on a local chicken bus in Nicaragua (as I did) and spend untold hours finding a replacement. The hunt for a good size 11 / 45 can be a long and arduous one.

Suggested clothing list

The following are some suggested sets of clothing intended to cover approximately a week's worth of use, and based on different weather conditions. You can, of course, adjust these examples based on your preferences.

Hot climate
- 7x underwear
- 2 pair of socks (there is no need for more as you'll probably be wearing flip flops or sandals much of the time)
- 4 t-shirts or tank tops
- 1 long-sleeve or button-up shirt

- 1 hoodie or jumper (you'll need this for air conditioned environments or when at higher elevations where it can be significantly colder)
- 1 pair of long trousers (based on your preference)
- 2 pairs of short leg-wear (men might opt for short trousers or cargo shorts, women also have the options of pack cut-off jeans and/or short dresses).
- Swimming gear
- Sunglasses
- Nightwear (don't overthink this for hot climates however – many end up sleeping in just sports- or boxer shorts along with a tank top or bikini)
- 1 pair of flip-flops or sandals
- 1 pair of good walking shoes

Temperate climate
- 7x underwear
- 7 pairs of socks
- 3 t-shirts
- 2 long-sleeve or button up shirts
- 1 hoodie or jumper
- 2x pairs of long trousers
- Coat
- Nightwear
- 1 pair of walking shoes
- 1 alternate footwear option (e.g. some canvas sneakers)

Cold climate
- *All of the above plus...*
- Scarf, hat, mittens, etc.
- Long-johns or heat tech undergarment
- Wind breaker jacket
- 1 pair of warm comfortable boots
- 1 alternate pair of footwear

The above lists are somewhat biased towards the male traveller; if you are female you will want to make some obvious additions and changes (such as adding bras).

Needless to say if your trip involves travelling only in one climate, pack only for this climate. A single-country or regional trip often has the benefit of giving you a fairly consistent weather situation across the board. Round-the-world travellers will instead be faced with having to potentially cover many different weather scenarios. If your trip is less about regional overland travel and more about hopping from continent to continent, you may have to compromise on the minimalism somewhat. Still, to cover multiple climates you might not need more than a couple of additional kilograms of clothing.

Air-conditioning: not always your friend

Even in tropical countries you will, at times, still be thankful for having a warm jumper or sweater with you. That's not only because of colder higher altitude areas. Air-conditioning is often considered a luxury in hot countries, and so to provide the 'best service' it sometimes gets cranked up to truly arctic levels. Cinemas in South- and Southeast Asia can be utterly freezing; don't watch a movie any longer than two hours or you will certainly die of frostbite. Buses in South America will sometimes set the AC to ridiculous levels—even to a point where, bizarrely, the locals will actually cover themselves in wool blankets to stay warm. Bring at least one warm and comfy layer with you, even if the climate doesn't seem to require it.

Do I really need...?

Besides clothing and footwear, what else should you pack? I believe it's best to make your own packing list based on your specific trip, so rather than providing a boilerplate list, let's just look at some common travel items and discuss their usefulness (or lack thereof).

Universal Travel adaptor—Verdict: YES!

This is surely the most useful gadget ever made. Universal travel adaptors are capable of transforming into any kind of plug type, ensuring that you can get always a charge anywhere in the world. Some universal adaptors also have USB ports, allowing you to charge multiple devices or batteries at once.

Flashlight—Verdict: YES (BUT...)

It can be tough finding your way in the dark in poorly lit places and some countries regularly suffer from power cuts, so it's a great idea to bring a flashlight. Night buses also often shut their lights early and may not have reading lights.

A regular flashlight might well suffice (as could a flashlight app on your smartphone, though these do drain the battery quickly). But better yet, bring a small LED head torch. These allow you to a shine a light on things while still having both your hands available. This is ideal for reading, digging through your backpack in the dark, or for use on caving or night hikes.

Light-weight microfiber travel towel—Verdict: YES!

Everything Douglas Adams ever wrote about towels is true. Don't leave home without one! Many backpacker hostels (and some budget hotels or guesthouses) do not offer towels. You could bring a regular towel, though they are heavy and slow to dry. Ultralight towels don't feel as nice to the touch but they dry more quickly and take up very little space. These towels can be very difficult to buy abroad, so this is an item you will probably want to purchase while at home.

As a side note, your towel will easily get stinky if you have to store it in your luggage before it has had a chance to dry properly. After showering it helps to wipe some of the water off your body with your hands first, before drying off the rest with your towel. This makes a noticeable difference in keeping your towel fresh and dry during a long journey. If your towel is still wet, store it somewhere away from your clothes.

Padlock—Verdict: YES!

Extremely useful if you are expecting at all to stay in backpacker hostels. Lockers are the main way to keep your belongings secure in hostels, and you'll be expected to use your own lock. Buy one with a combination lock so you don't have to worry about losing the key.

Antibacterial gel—Verdict: YES

Hygiene standards vary hugely around the world, and they are particularly poor in developing countries, so it's great to have this as a back-up. You may find yourself at a grungy bus station toilet without any soap, or you may want to clean your hands after petting any animals.

First aid kit—Verdict: YES, BUT...

There's no need to pack a huge first-aid box with enough supplies to patch up a whole platoon of wounded soldiers. It doesn't hurt to bring along a small first-aid kit, though. Some key items you may want to bring include plasters/Band-Aids, Ibuprofen (painkillers) and Imodium (anti-diarrhoea pills). Other items that could be useful include some gauze and some antiseptic cream. All of this should be able to fit inside a small kit or a single pocket in your bag. For anything beyond basic first aid, seek medical attention locally.

Obviously if you are on any specific prescriptions at home, make sure these medicines are available at your destination or bring an adequate supply.

Camera—Verdict: YES.

Essential for keeping memories of your trip. Whether you should go with a point-and-shoot or bring a bulky SLR camera depends on your level of enthusiasm for photography as well as your ability to use a camera well. An SLR doesn't automatically make your photos amazing; if you have never ventured outside of the AUTO setting it may be worth taking some photography classes first, or just sticking with a lighter and more compact camera for the occasional casual snaps. Phone cameras are beginning to rival the quality of some of the compact cameras out there, and so your camera phone may well be sufficient for your needs.

If you're serious about your photography, it might be a good idea to bring along a spare battery or two so you can keep shooting even through long days, or even in remote locations where you can't easily recharge the battery.

Tripod—Verdict: PROBABLY NOT.

If you are a semi-pro or enthusiast photographer and love using long exposures, or if you need photos to be razor sharp for commercial use, then a tripod is a great tool for you. Otherwise, it's probably not worth the hassle, even if using one makes you look more professional.

Water purifying tablets or UV purifiers—Verdict: NO.

Within the context of regular world travel, you will find that safe bottled drinking water is available virtually everywhere. The only scenario in which you may need purifying tablets is when going on adventurous and remote hiking expeditions (particularly self-organised ones, i.e. not with a guide or touring company, though this is beyond the expertise or ambition of many travellers). Do avoid drinking water from taps in developing countries as this can easily get you sick; buy bottled water in stores or get water from water-coolers where these are provided.

Piano—Verdict: HELL NO.

If you were thinking of travelling around the world with a 125kg piano, I hate to tell you that this has already been done. You can follow a German guy's ordeal of travelling the world with a huge piano at mytraveling-piano.com. If you need a travel instrument, I would perhaps suggest a ukulele.

Hammock—Verdict: NO (unless...)

The idea of bringing a hammock has an undeniable romantic attraction, but in practice they are only useful in very particular situations. Only few travellers who set out to sleep only in hammocks end up following through on this plan, especially when affordable accommodation is so easy to find in many places around the world.

A hammock can in some cases be a great tool if you seriously need to cut down on costs. If you are travelling on the shortest of shoe-strings, a hammock may occasionally enable you to sleep in gardens or on beaches (though this is not always the safest idea). Hammocks can also come in handy in the Amazon where they are used on the river boats, or in the rarely-visited and more expensive South American countries like French Guyana and Suriname, where you may wish to pay $10 for a place to hang your hammock instead of forking out $70 a night for a hotel.

These are special-case scenarios though, so unless you have some specifically in mind, a hammock will probably to take up space needlessly. Some ultralight hammocks do compress down to a bag about the size of a large apple, so these can be a good choice if you only need a hammock for occasional opportunistic use.

Sewing Kit—Verdict: NOT ESSENTIAL.

This comes up in packing lists all the time, but there seem to be only limited opportunities to use this. Worn clothes can be replaced, and minor repairs are so rare as to not require a dedicated sewing kit.

Swiss army knife or multi-tool—Verdict: MEH

This has some limited utility, though knives can also prevent you from flying with carry-on luggage only as they are usually not allowed on board. If some MacGuyvering is required on your trip, see if you can borrow tools from the hostel or hotel you are staying. The manager, janitor, or cleaner probably has just the thing you need.

Mosquito net—Verdict: NO.

Broadly speaking, a mosquito net is not required for conventional independent travel. Sleeping arrangements where mosquito nets are necessary, such as in jungle huts or home-stays in remote villages, will typically already have them. One exception can be sub-Saharan Africa, as this is the world's highest-risk region for malaria. Having your own mosquito net may be a worthwhile investment for travel here, though do check if this is actually recommended by travel guides for your specific destination(s) in Africa. In other parts of the world, a mosquito net is more likely to be a waste of money and space.

(Admittedly this is still a bit of a generalization. Exceptions may also include some of the more remote parts of the world, such as the heart of the Amazon, the backwaters of Borneo or the furthest reaches of Papua New Guinea. These are not places people easily end up in, and so mosquito nets should not be a concern for the vast majority of travellers. Though even when targeting these remote areas with any sort of predictable purpose, for instance to see Urang Utangs on Borneo or to scuba dive in Papua New Guinea, you are likely to end up in areas that do regularly see visitors and where mosquito nets or screens are taken care of.)

Mosquito repellent—Verdict: YES

This comes in very handy particularly when travelling in tropical destinations. Be sure to get repellent containing DEET. Many lotions and sprays have 10% or higher DEET content, with a concentration of around 50% usually the highest available. Mosquito repellent is widely available everywhere, though not always at the higher tropical strengths, so you may want to buy a bottle at home. Some countries, for instance Malaysia, only allow the sale of weaker citronella-based repellent.

Umbrella—Verdict: NO.

Bulky, so leave at home. Bring a plastic poncho or a lightweight rain jacket if you need any rain cover.

Earplugs—Verdict: YES.

Essential. Blocks out the noise from bus and train engines, snorers, street noise, and long-winded travel stories.

It's best to buy some good ones at home; while you can buy extra earplugs at a local pharmacy or supermarket while on the road, the quality can sometimes leave much to be desired. (For instance, I struggled to find good earplugs anywhere in the Andes.)

Foam earplugs are the most common and provide good noise reduction. A nifty newer type of earplug is made of soft silicone, which you can mould with your fingers and then insert in your ear, enclosing it perfectly.

Travel pillow—Verdict: MAYBE.

If you need to rest your head while in transit, rolling up a hoodie can turn this into a not-entirely-terrible improvised pillow. If you want something a little better, get an inflatable travel pillow that weighs little and is easy to store.

Sleeping bag—Verdict: NO.

Absolutely not needed. Even the lowest-budget accommodation will offer bed sheets and covers. Unless you plan on sleeping in a tent, leave your sleeping bag at home.

There are admittedly some very rare exceptions of youth hostels in Europe and North America with rock-bottom prices not offering bedding, but generally speaking a sleeping bag is not at all necessary.

If your main concern is just to have a layer between you and any bed-sheets provided, bring a sleeping bag liner. This is much lighter than a full sleeping bag and can easily act as an extra layer of bedding if needed.

Sarong: better than a Swiss army knife

A sarong (or any kind of large cloth) is a neat multi-purpose travel accessory that you might not need to pack now, but which you can potentially buy during your trip. Sarongs are typically used as a skirt, but they can be so much more. Need a picnic blanket? You've got one. Going to the beach? There's your beach mat. Need a nap? Just wrap some clothes in your sarong, tie it up, and you will have fashioned yourself a primitive pillow. Too hot? Turn it into a bandana. Too cold? You have a scarf. Not bad for just a single item.

Packing and organization tips

You have probably noticed this chapter's mantra of "less is more". Beyond what's been already discussed, there are a few other ways to reduce packing weight and volume.

When it comes to toiletries, pare down the number of gels, crèmes, and so on. Women usually bring a more basic set of make-up than they use at home. Many toiletries are available in a convenient smaller travel size, which have the added bonus of being allowed as part of carry-on luggage on flights.

One thing to note for women is that sanitary items (particularly tampons) are not common in some countries, especially Muslim countries. This is more of a problem in remote areas rather than in cities, but it may be wise to bring a supply.

Try to minimize the number of electronic devices you bring. These can be bulky and each come with different wires, batteries and adaptors, which can add clutter fast.

Don't feel the need to bring a whole library of books with you, even if you think you will need a lot of reading material on your trip. In traveller hubs (i.e. places that many people pass through) you will typically find second-hand book stores where you can pick up a good read. Larger cities and airports have international book stores where you can buy books in many languages, and many hostels have book exchanges where you can top up your reading material as well.

Of course, you can eliminate a lot of weight by bringing an e-book reader. It's perhaps a more theft-sensitive item than a book (you have to look out for it more when taking it to a beach, for instance), but it's hard to beat their ultra-low weight and versatility.

A few other ways to minimize weight (or maximize your available space):

- Wear your bulkiest shoes whenever you are moving between places, so that you don't have to keep them in your bag.
- Shoes can also be tied to the outside of your bag by their laces.
- Avoid buying too many souvenirs, at least until the final stages of your trip. You don't want to buy a ton of (big or heavy) souvenirs when you still have months of travel left to go.
- Don't bring a guidebook for a country you won't be visiting until much later. You can usually buy new or used guidebooks in major cities, or find used guidebooks in book exchanges or second-hand stores. Sell or exchange guidebooks when you no longer need them. Many hostels have travel guides that you can browse which may well suffice for your research needs; you can even take pictures of maps and other details using your phone.
- You can send home any stuff you are no longer using. For instance, if you have just left a cold climate, box up your scarves, mittens, snowmobile, etc. and send it back. If you will still be travelling for a while, you can make perfect use of some slow but also very cheap shipping options.

Try to leave at least a quarter of your bag empty, for easier packing and unpacking (and for potentially storing souvenirs, gifts or other additional items you buy along the way). If packing your bag feels like an advanced game of Tetris, your bag is definitely too full.

For separating and organizing your bag's contents, a basic and free method is to simply use some shopping- or tote bags. There are however many products on the market specifically designed for organizing or compressing your luggage.

Packing cubes and stuff sacks can help you keep your belongings organized, in particular soft items like your clothing. If you do use these, be sure to avoid overly-large-sized ones (as they encourage you to fill them) and if you use more than one, ensure that they have different colours (making it easier to differentiate between them).

Compression bags are a neat solution for 'deep storage'. They can reduce the volume of clothes by up to 80% by letting excess air out through a special valve. It is not very practical to take items in and out of a compression bag all the time, so you wouldn't want to use one for things you need every day. However, it can save you a lot of space when storing items longer-term. For instance, you can compress your cold climate clothes when travelling in a hot climate.

Transparent zip-lock bags are useful for keeping smaller items organized, such as small toiletries or camera accessories and batteries. Zip-lock bags can also serve as basic dry bags for your passport or other key items that you don't want to accidentally get wet.

It's a good precaution to put any liquids (such as shampoo or body wash) in a separate bag or container as leakage accidents can happen during transit. Finding your bag entirely drenched in soap because a cap came unscrewed can make you a grumpy traveller.

Packing and unpacking: how not to lose stuff

Since you will probably be on the move again every few days, it's good to stick to a regular packing regimen. Find a suitable place for each item and then try to keep it there throughout your journey. For instance, instead of putting that electrical adaptor in a different pocket every time, designate one pocket as the adaptor pocket. This makes it easier to find things, and easier to conduct a quick survey of your bag before checking out of your hotel.

If you need to get up and leave in the early morning, it's better to pack your bag the night before; it's easy to lose things when it's dark or when you are still half-asleep. This is doubly true when staying in dorms as other people's items may be scattered around the room which can easily lead to mistakes. I once lost my favourite t-shirt and gained some random women's underwear only because I had packed hastily in a poorly lit dormitory.

Always do a double take before you leave your room: check your bed, check the floor, check the bathroom. When travelling for many weeks or months on end, chances are that you will lose something somewhere down the line, but you can significantly reduce these chances by getting into this habit.

Digital devices

There are clearly many benefits to bringing a computer or smartphone on your trip, whether it's for staying connected, typing up travel journals, copying and editing photos, or simply having some entertainment during long journeys.

Of course, it is also perfectly possible to travel without a computer, tablet or other digital device; in fact, you could argue that staying away from the digital world can help you immerse in your journey all the more. Going analogue for a while, and staying far away from all the Facebooks and Instagrams of this world, can give you a chance to reboot and recharge. Turning a trip into a digital-free retreat is not for everyone though, and many people end up bringing at least one digital device with them on their journey.

A smartphone is the obvious device to bring along, as it's ideally sized and covers all your basic travel needs. Whether you want to go beyond this and take a more fully-featured tablet or laptop on the road depends on your specific needs.

For instance, do you need to work online while abroad? Do you need to easily process and edit photos or video files? Is it essential that you have a bigger screen or a larger keyboard? These are some of the questions you will have to ask yourself. You may well decide that bringing additional electronics with you is essential, especially if you aspire to be a location-independent digital nomad, or if you simply don't want to be without your own computer in the time that you'll be away.

What follows are some brief thoughts on each category of digital device, their pros and cons for travel use, and some tips on getting the most use out of them.

Load up some travel apps to make bookings and trip planning easier.

Smartphones

A smartphone clearly does the job just fine for basic email, Skype, music, internet browsing, and so on. They can also easily function as your travel camera so long as you don't have too high demands in terms of lens quality or pixel resolution (at least, when compared to a dedicated SLR or a good compact camera).

One thing to keep in mind when taking your expensive smartphone travelling is that they can be easy to lose. People tend to keep items such as laptops, cameras and tablets securely stored in their bags or in a locker, whereas they often handle their phone with much less care. By now I have heard far too many stories of lost or stolen phones (and I myself once stupidly lost an iPhone in the jungles of Laos), so this is one item to keep a watchful eye on. Keep in mind that, to a local living in some of the world's poorer countries, a latest model iPhone or Samsung Galaxy may well be worth many months of wages, so it's best not to be too flashy with them and to look after them well.

If you don't want to bring your top-of-the-line smartphone, you could always go lower-tech. Before I went off to go backpacking for a year in Latin America (where I knew crime levels are relatively high) I decided I did not want to risk losing another $600+ device, as I had done previously in Laos. So instead I purchased a cheap $70 smartphone by a relatively unknown Chinese manufacturer. It was far too slow to play any games or to run many apps at the same time, but it did the job just fine for listening to podcasts or music, checking my email, or looking up travel info. When I eventually (and stupidly) left this phone on a bus in Colombia, I still managed to trace it back thanks to a helpful local. The sheer undesirability of this phone may have had something to do with actually getting it back and not having it stolen, though of course I will never know. Either way, I would have shed significantly less tears if I had in fact been lost. Going with a deliberately crappy phone may not at all be necessary (I was clearly overly paranoid after I had lost one phone already), but it's an option that's there.

If the internet or media functions of a smartphone are not essential to you (or you already have these functions covered by another device), and you just want to have a phone for calls or for emergency purposes, there is also always the option of getting a feature phone for a mere $20 or so. It will of course only do basic calls and texts, but its battery will last seemingly forever. (Remember when a mobile phone could run on a single charge for a whole month? Crazy.)

Having said all that, realistically most travellers will simply bring whatever smartphone device they already own.

If your smartphone is going to be your main device, there are some clever ways in which you can extend its functionality. Firstly, if you have an Android phone you can pair it with a portable hard drive via USB. Accessing the drive via the phone might require formatting this hard drive in the FAT32 format (as not all Android phones can read drives in other formats like NTFS). This may take a little bit of looking into, but if you can get this to work you will be able to dramatically increase the storage space of your phone. You can then store entire libraries of media well beyond what will fit onto an SD card, or you can use the drive as a secondary storage location for your travel photos and such. Combining a phone with a small portable hard-drive is obviously a very compact set-up that's perfect for travel.

If you need to do a lot of writing, you can also pair a phone with a Bluetooth keyboard. This isn't exactly an ideal set-up, but it can be a low-budget way of gaining some basic word processing functionality on the go, if this is something you need. Basic portable Bluetooth keyboards cost as little as $10 - $20. Some keyboards are even made of flexible material and can be rolled up for storage in your backpack.

Laptops

If you are going on a long journey, or you expect to travel regularly, you may want to look into specifically bringing a laptop that's both capable and lightweight. There are different categories of laptop to consider for travel. Broadly speaking, you've got mini-laptops and Chromebooks on the budget end, and ultrabooks on the higher end of the market.

Chromebooks are a perfect low-budget option allowing you to do most (but not quite all) things on the go. You can find many small 11" or 12" Chromebooks for just around $200. Do make sure you understand what a Chromebook is: they are designed to be used primarily while connected to the internet using Google's Chrome OS, with files mainly stored in the cloud and most apps being web-based. While they do allow offline work as well via Chrome Apps that are made for this purpose, Chromebooks are still essentially designed to be "dumb' machines that connect to smart servers via the internet, and so they are typically very light on processing power and memory. Most Chromebooks have just 16GB of storage space, which can be a little restrictive. They are good for word processing and internet use, but not that great for photo or video editing.

Alternatively, there are small 11" mini laptops out there running Windows, also costing somewhere around $200 while being similarly low-spec. Both this category of laptop and Chromebooks are reasonably light, typically weighing somewhere around 1.2kg.

On the higher end you've got ultrabooks, truly the ultimate tool for the long-term drifter or digital nomad. While relatively expensive, they are simply unbeatable in terms of battery life, weight and functionality. Macbook Air established the category and continues to lead the pack, with the lowest weight, best battery life, and greatest ease of use (but, not surprisingly given that this is Apple, also the biggest price tag). I travel with a Macbook Air nowadays and love having a computer with me that's fully-featured and also delivers 12+ hours of battery life. As a blogger and remote worker, it's become my most essential tool.

Many PC manufacturers make ultrabooks with specs similar to the Macbook Air. There are also cheaper models, for instance by ASUS and Acer, though these tend to make compromises that make them less ideal for mobile use. For instance, a cheaper ASUS Ultrabook will weigh more, have less battery life (e.g. 3 hours instead of 12) and may only have a small caching SSD instead of a full SSD drive. I travelled with an ASUS laptop for a while and was significantly less pleased, as it seemed to sit awkwardly in between a real ultra-book and some of the cheaper options out there.

Tablets

Tablets are wonderfully portable, though they can sometimes lack utility or convenience while travelling. Tablets that work well as a coffee table or reading device for the home may not work quite as well during long-term travels.

iPads are particularly troublesome (and I once travelled with one for 8 months). Its initial appeal as a travel device is obvious: its battery life is phenomenal, it's incredibly light-weight, and it covers all your basic functions. But you might also run into some frustrations. For instance, to import photos you have to manually tap them one by one, making it a poor camera companion. If you want to watch your own video files on an iPad you often have to convert them to mp4 format before uploading them through iTunes, which takes a while. As a relatively closed system, it's also difficult to get files on and off the iPad, and difficult to share files with other travellers.

Arguably, Android tablets are more versatile for travel than iPads, mainly because they allow the use of external storage locations. The tip mentioned earlier of pairing a smartphone with a portable hard drive of course also goes for Android tablets.

A tablet can still be a great travel device, especially if you don't need the sort of productivity functions offered by a laptop.

Packing your digital things—movies, music, etc.

While this chapter is all about being minimalist when packing, you can take the complete opposite approach with anything digital. Whether it's e-books, TV shows, movies, podcasts or music, stock up on as much material as you can. If you are going to be taking a lot of long overland journeys, it's nice to have a generous supply of entertainment to keep you busy. It's far easier to download or transfer these materials at home while you still have reliable internet.

Using public computers

Finally, one other option is to use public computers in internet cafés or in hostels and hotels whenever you have the opportunity. If all you need is to write a longer email sometimes or update a blog occasionally, this can be a perfect substitute for bringing a computer or tablet of your own.

One terrible aspect of public computers however is that they always have the wrong language or keyboard settings, often have all sorts of confusing toolbars installed, and are vulnerable to viruses and malware. Using a PC at an internet cafe is not really like having the familiar environment of your own computer. Always unticking the "remember me" box when logging into a site and having to always log out are some other little annoyances.

One neat trick that addresses this issue (at least partially) is bringing a USB stick loaded with a portable version of your favourite browser. You can download versions of browsers like Chrome that are specially modified to run from a USB stick at www.portableapps.com. Once you have this, simply stick the USB drive into any computer, run the browser on it, and you immediately have all your bookmarks, settings, logins, and other personalizations ready to go. This is a lot nicer than wrestling with a browser in an internet café that has 5 different search toolbars installed and its language set to Swahili.

Portable apps will even run from any storage device, so conceivably you can even put them on your phone or camera's SD memory card. Just connect this device to a PC with a USB cable, and then run the application by double clicking it in Windows Explorer. It's just one more creative idea that might allow you to leave your other bulkier digital devices at home.

Bring some good music

Speaking of all things digital, special mention should be made for bringing some music along on your trip, as the music you listen to will inevitably become deeply associated with your journey. Bring your favourite tunes or some new material you know you will love. A quick way to stock up on some additional travel music is to subscribe to Spotify (or a similar service) and follow playlists with names such as "mood: travelling" or "road trip music".

Soundtracks can make for great listening material as well. When I first went to Tokyo I listened to the soundtrack of *Lost in Translation*, enhancing my Tokyo experience immeasurably. When riding the Pacific Express through the Copper Canyon in Mexico I happened to listen to the soundtrack of *Red Dead Redemption*, a video game set in the Wild West. When the main theme came on I nearly shed a tear, as it fit so perfectly with the desert landscapes passing me by. There may be cool soundtracks to think of for the places you are going as well.

Key points from this chapter

- Pack light.
- ***PACK LIGHT!!!*** *(ROAR!!!)*
- A good way to force yourself to pack light is to **use a smaller backpack**.
- **Be wary of overly lengthy packing lists.** A lot of them are just trying to be the most complete instead of paring it down to the essentials. Many packing lists are for wilderness hiking and not for travelling.

- **Invest in a good quality backpack** if you haven't already. This will reward you with increased comfort throughout your trip.
- **Bring footwear that's appropriate** to your needs and your destination.
- The most important items to bring are your passport and visas (if any), driving license, and bank and credit cards. Look after them carefully.
- Reduce everything else until you are left with only the bare minimum.
- If you're considering bringing a **computer, tablet or other digital devices,** make sure you will actually need them.
- Don't worry too much about forgetting a non-essential item. **You can always buy it there.**
- When it comes to bringing anything that's digital, the sky is the limit! Load up as much movies, music, ebooks, and other files as you think you'll need.

[7]

Buying travel insurance

IN SOME SENSE, buying travel insurance (or not buying it) is a gamble. You don't want to ever regret not buying the insurance, but you also don't want to pay for something you don't need. Maybe this is why there's often much debate among travellers about whether to get insured—even though there really shouldn't be.

If in doubt, err on the side of caution and get yourself insured.

Conceivably there are some low-risk scenarios where travel insurance is not essential. For instance, you might be on a cultural city trip where you'll be spending most of your time in museums and restaurants; maybe you are not as likely to run into major issues there. Or you might be visiting a country that neighbours your own and from which you could easily come back in an emergency. If your trip has a more limited scope, maybe the chances of anything going wrong are remote enough for insurance not to be worth the cost.

But when you're travelling far and wide, and especially when you're going to adventurous countries or partaking in adventurous activities (things like sports, hiking, zip-lining, or climbing), it makes a lot of sense to get comprehensive travel insurance. This won't, in itself, help you stay safe or healthy, but it can minimize the considerable financial risks of travelling, particularly in the case of accidents or other unforeseen situations.

Of course, most likely nothing will happen at all on your trip, but problems do occur. To give just one example, I once met someone who had gotten into a motorbike accident and had to be treated in a hospital, but because he was uninsured he had to go into debt to pay his hospital bills. He had to cancel the rest of his trip, and was stuck in one place just trying to get enough money together to fly back home. Eventualities like these, while rare, do happen—and so it's best to be prepared for them. The scenario I have just painted could of course have been much worse.

Despite what some may claim, travel insurance is far from an unnecessary luxury; it's a must-have for any serious world traveller. It's a relatively minor expense, but it can give you a lot of peace of mind. Even if you doubt the need for it yourself, it can give peace of mind to any loved ones you have at home, who may have a very different perception of the risks or dangers of world travel.

Finding the right insurance can be a bit of a mission. The needs of a long-term traveller are different from those going on a brief holiday. And, as we'll see, there are many types of coverage that a long-term traveller could actually do without. Where you are going matters as well, as some regions or continents may not be covered by default or may require an additional premium.

Keep in mind that your existing medical insurance at home most likely will not cover you abroad. Regular medical insurance typically offers domestic coverage only, which is why you will need the additional travel insurance for any potential medical expenses abroad.

Basic terminology explained

It's possible you never had to deal with insurance before, so here is the unabashedly basic explanation: insurance is a system by which you pay a specified amount to the insurer, which in turn gives you a certain level of coverage. This means that if something then were to happen (e.g. loss, damage, illness) and it's within your coverage, the insurer will have to compensate you financially.

For instance, if you become ill and need to see a doctor, you can file a claim with your insurer. Usually this requires sending them a doctor's report and other details supporting your claim. If the insurer finds nothing unusual about your claim and has checked that it's within your coverage, they will compensate you according to the amount specified in your policy.

Insurance usually has a specified "excess". An excess is an amount of money you will have to pay yourself if you decide to claim on your policy. So if your excess for medical expenses is €50, and the treatment you received cost €200, you can only claim back only €150. It is not always that simple however: the excess for stolen items could be per item rather than taken together, so read your policy well, as the devil is always in the details.

It is often possible to buy an upgraded insurance package with a lower or even no excess, though this will come at a higher cost (also called a higher "premium").

Before you buy travel insurance

When setting out to buy travel insurance, be sure to follow these steps first:

1. Check if you already have insurance

You may already be covered without realizing, as some credit cards and bank accounts offer annual travel insurance as a free bonus. It's also possible that another family member has got you covered as part of a family travel insurance package. Do check if the existing insurance covers you for long stay travel or for the specific countries or activities you are planning.

2. Check if your existing travel insurance covers long trips

Perhaps you already have an annual travel insurance policy for your regular holidays. Keep in mind though that most standard annual packages have a limit on the length of a single trip. In many cases this is 30 days, though sometimes it is 60 or 90 days. Depending on the length of your trip, your existing insurance might not be adequate, so make sure you check the maximum length of stay for any existing policy you have.

3. Look for backpacker or long stay travel insurance

There are countless insurers catering specifically to globe trotters and adventure travellers, offering both annual and single-trip packages. Some backpacker insurance policies even give you the flexibility to extend them while on your trip, should you want to travel longer than planned. They usually also include coverage for outdoors activities or adventure sports, and sometimes also cover working or volunteering abroad. Search around for "backpacker insurance" or "long stay travel insurance".

Essential coverage

Listing specific insurers or insurance packages here won't be of much help, as this is very changeable in nature. It also gets complicated fast, as different insurers operate in different markets.

While I can't tell you exactly what sort of travel insurance is right for you, I can perhaps help point towards types of coverage to look out for if you're going on a big journey, based on personal experience and opinion.

Many travel insurance packages offer all kinds of bells and whistles that frankly aren't so essential if you are not on a more conventional holiday. The two most important things to look for are coverage for medical expenses and personal liability.

Personal Liability insurance will be a real life saver if you accidentally damage someone's property or accidentally injure someone. So if you happen to, say, walk through a luxury mansion and accidentally knock down an insanely expensive antique Chinese vase (just a ridiculous example), it doesn't have to bankrupt you for the rest of your life. Personal liability is usually covered up to a significant amount (often a million or above).

Medical coverage speaks for itself and is essential for any traveller. It is not just useful in the case of severe illness or accident but also for smaller unforeseen medical issues. Perhaps you will need some emergency dental treatment or be treated for an allergic reaction. I once got inner-ear barotrauma after a week of intense scuba diving and was glad to be able to get some free specialist check-ups. While some will argue that medical treatment is relatively cheap in many non-Western countries, bills can still add up quickly if you need to see a doctor multiple times.

Most insurers will cover you for up to millions of Dollars/Euros/Pounds of medical expenses. This is a somewhat hypothetical number, but the point is that should any legitimate medical emergency occur you will most likely not have to worry about the cost, so long as you can make proper claims. Do check if the insurer covers pre-existing conditions and be sure to disclose any you might have, as failing to do so can invalidate claims even if the pre-existing condition is completely unrelated.

If repatriation to your home country is necessary, this is almost always also covered. In serious cases additional accommodation or travel expenses can sometimes also be claimed.

Be sure to closely examine which sports or activities are covered. Policies will have a list of what is and what isn't. These lists contain all sorts of obscure and at times surprising activities. For example, my insurer covers husky sledge driving, falconing, and archaeological digging, but I would have to pay a premium for playing American football, riding ostriches or partaking in historical battle re-enactments. (Who knew insurance policies could be such a good source of bucket list inspiration?)

Unless you are planning to engage in particularly injury-prone activities, the standard list will usually have you covered. Activities like hiking, mountain biking, snorkelling, surfing, scuba diving (up to 30 or 40m, the usual limit for recreational diving) as well as various common sports should be expected in any standard package with a reputable insurer.

World Nomads: not the only travel insurer!

If you look online for tips about backpacker travel insurance, you will no doubt find many blogs recommending World Nomads, a company that's also endorsed by Lonely Planet. This insurer is, in fact, very good. Their level of service is very high—but so is their price. One reason that World Nomads gets recommended a lot is that they run a successful affiliate program, meaning that travel blogs get a little bit of commission from any customers they refer to them. While they are definitely a good option, they are far from the only player around—and others may offer similar packages at more competitive prices. It's always worth shopping around.

Additional types of coverage

Besides medical expenses or personal liability, a travel insurance package may also cover a range of other situations. Some of these are more important than others. Here are some of the common ones, along with my personal view as to how relevant these are:

Theft

Perhaps controversially, I would call this a "nice to have" rather than an essential. Coverage for theft often seems better than it is, and the devil is in the details. The terms may say that your valuables are covered up to a certain amount, but the contractual definition of valuables may (somewhat bizarrely) exclude items such as cameras or mobile phones that are more commonly lost. Be sure to check out the fine print.

If you watch your things closely and use some of the common anti-theft precautions, you should be okay without theft insurance. Most backpackers don't carry fortunes worth of stuff around anyway, so the potential financial damage is limited. If you do carry some very expensive items with you, they usually require an additional premium to insure.

The claims process may in some cases also be more trouble than it's worth. For instance, it usually requires obtaining a police report which can be a bureaucratic ordeal in the more remote places.

And, of course, there is usually a standard excess (typically in the €50 to €100 range on standard packages), so if any stolen items are below this value you won't get compensated at all.

Keep in mind that to make a claim for a lost or stolen item you will always need some proof of ownership, such as an original receipt.

Loss of passport

Again, this is certainly nice to have, but not essential. Should you lose your passport, you will have to go to your country's embassy or consulate and pay for a replacement. This can cost around, say, a hundred dollar or euros, which is definitely unfortunate but not the largest financial setbacks you could imagine. While nice, this is not the main reason to get insurance.

Cancellation

Cancellation coverage means you will be compensated in the event that you have to cancel your trip for specific emergency reasons for any booking or cancellation fees. This is not hugely relevant if you are travelling long-term, as you will be more likely booking accommodation and transportation as you need them and not all in advance.

Curtailment

This entitles you to some financial compensation if you need to go home early for an emergency, such as a death in the family. If you are travelling independently, there is less risk of losing money through cancellations as you won't be booking ahead as much as someone who's on a tightly scripted holiday. If you have a flexible return ticket, your return flight can often be changed for a booking amendment fee. This can be up to around €100 depending on the terms and conditions. This is, broadly speaking, a limited financial risk.

Missed Departure

Allows compensation if you miss your flight due to circumstances such as a traffic accident, bad weather, public transportation failure, etc. Usually this only covers your flight to and from home.

Scheduled Airline Failure

Applies only in the case of an airline going bankrupt; a rare scenario.

# # #

While none of the items above are absolutely critical, they are of course nice to have as part of a comprehensive insurance package. The point is that when you are evaluating insurance options, they should not be the main things to compare. Medical and personal liability coverage are typically the main reasons to take travel insurance.

If you are thinking of taking a particularly expensive item with you (for example a professional-quality camera or lens) and you are concerned about loss or damage, you could insure this item separately. Regular insurance packages usually have an individual item limit which means part of the value of expensive items (perhaps almost all of it) falls outside of your coverage, so separately insuring a highly valuable item may be worth the premium for the increased ease of mind.

Key points from this chapter

- Travel insurance can be **a real life-saver** if you get into trouble.
- **Look for good medical and personal liability coverage in particular.**
- Theft coverage usually has limitations you need to be aware of; **be sure to read the fine print**. Expensive items such as electronics may not be covered in full, especially in the more affordable insurance packages out there.
- Many insurers offer **insurance specifically tailored to RTW or backpacker travellers.** This will for instance cover more sports and activities, or their duration can be extended while you are travelling should you want to travel longer than planned.

[8]

Personal safety and security

ANYONE WHO HAS EVER been on an airplane will know that all-too-familiar phrase from the pre-flight safety instructions: "in the unlikely event..."

Even though air travel is, by all statistical accounts, one of the safest methods to travel, merely raising the ever-so-distant possibility of a crash can still give you the creeps.

It's often the same with information about the safety or security situation in different countries. There's clearly some stuff you need to know, some things that need to be mentioned, but doing so can maybe make you a little uncomfortable. This chapter, too, will have a few mentions of "unlikely events".

When I get questions about travel safety from readers of my blog, I often find these the most difficult to answer. When I'm writing a response, I inevitably get into a tug-of-war with myself between not wanting to needlessly exacerbate any fears but also wanting to tell people not to be naive.

I believe there are two basic truths about travel safety:

Truth No. 1: The world is not as scary as it might seem. It's easy to build up completely inaccurate stereotypes of the safety situation in other countries. The news might make you believe the world is full of terrorists and explosions... but actually, by and large, not so much. Travelling the world can really open your eyes to how different places are to how you might imagine them from a distance. Travel can even give you an amazing trust in humanity, as even in the seemingly grittiest places you will find the friendliest and most helpful people. Countless people travel the world for years (or even indefinitely) without ever experiencing any serious issues at all.

Truth No. 2: Nevertheless, you shouldn't be naive. While people are often disproportionately worried about travel safety, that doesn't mean that travel doesn't come with *some* risk. To be a responsible traveller, it's necessary to be well-informed and to always maintain some situational awareness. If you do anything willy-nilly without any care for your personal safety or security, your risks will be far greater than when you travel armed with proper knowledge and a sensible attitude.

In the end, striking a balance between being careful and embracing adventure is key. While healthy vigilance is good, constant paranoia is not.

Finding your comfort level

Safety is not just about the objective reality on the ground, but it's also about how safe you *feel*.

If you have relatively little travel experience you might approach some parts of the world with less confidence, even though they are safe enough for you to go to.

Your appetite for going to less familiar places will probably depend on where you are as a traveller. It's easier to go to Amsterdam and feel totally comfortable about your surroundings, than to go to Rio de Janeiro where the city centre is quite safe but where many of the outer barrios and favelas are definitely bad news (and which the responsible traveller will know to avoid).

Sometimes it helps to have travelled in more familiar places before going into less familiar territory. Over time, the seasoned traveller will develop a higher tolerance for unfamiliarity and a greater comfort level in places that maybe look a little run down (but which doesn't necessarily say anything about the safety level of a place).

Some dangers are more obvious than others...

Countries in the developed world, such as the United States, Canada, Japan, members of the European Union, Australia and New Zealand, are very safe and you should not think twice about travelling there. Keep in mind, they are not utopian and crime does happen (and some specific cities are known for high crime levels), but you can clearly be more at ease in all of the more advanced economies.

The majority of countries in the middle-income and developing world are also very safe, or at least sufficiently safe for travellers. As long as you apply common sense and navigate these countries responsibly, you will find that personal safety is rarely a real issue.

What's always key, however, is to research the safety situation in a country you intend to visit. This will allow you to avoid key trouble-spots if necessary or, in some cases, avoid a country entirely if it is not recommended to travel there currently.

Don't make assumptions either way. Your research might tell you to avoid places, or it might actually also tell you the situation is much better than you might have thought. Some countries used to get a bad rap but have improved dramatically in recent times. For instance, Colombia used to be closely associated only with bad things, but it is a much-loved backpacking destination today (but where common sense care still applies, of course).

Don't go into conflict zones (of course...)

Some countries are justifiably known as dangerous. Unless getting shot at by guerrillas or dying from mortar fire are high on your bucket list, active conflict zones don't make for ideal travel destinations. And unless you undergo extensive hazardous environment training and bring along a security team, you may not want to go backpacking in unstable countries like Iraq, Yemen, the Democratic Republic of Congo or Somalia. As old maps used to say, "Here be dragons". The advice in this chapter applies only to countries where the political situation is stable.

How to read a safety advisory

General safety information is available from travel guides or from reputable online guides. For more up-to-date information, including any updates based on recent developments, you should check the travel advisories on your State Department or Ministry of Foreign Affairs' website.

Take these travel advisories seriously but don't let them make you paranoid either, as they are typically overly alarmist. They are often colour coded and very little has to happen for a country to be given a big red flag. Unless you read them with the right mind-set, you could easily be deterred from visiting a country that is perfectly fine for you to visit.

For example: looking at the advisories for Thailand, the first thing I see is a red triangular warning sign with an exclamation mark, which certainly gets my attention. It says the political situation is currently "relatively stable" but there's "still potential for political unrest", and that I should avoid being near demonstrations of any kind. I am also told that areas along the Malaysian border are labelled as "no go" due to potential military skirmishes.

Demonstrations? No go areas? Military skirmishes? Sounds like a hot mess! Who in their right mind would go there? And yet millions of tourists go to Thailand every year, and anyone who has been will attest that it is indeed a very safe country.

Of course, technically everything in the advisory is true. Thailand suffers from occasionally turbulent politics. There is a low-intensity conflict in the remote province of Pattani near the Malaysian border, though this region is rarely visited by tourists, and you should simply heed the advice and not go there. Not that you would get past the security checkpoints anyway.

This is a key issue with travel advisories: often the warnings are about some easily avoidable specific areas, while the rest of the country is just fine. Your takeaway, more often than not, should be "right, so I clearly shouldn't go to that sketchy area", and not necessarily write off the entire country as a whole.

Keep in mind that a government travel advisory will never tell you "it's mostly just fine to go here, go on then and have a good time". There would clearly be repercussions for the government if someone very unlucky *does* run into trouble after reading that. So think of travel advisories as coming from someone who desperately does not want to get sued. Consider also that travel advisories are not just written for tourists but also for diplomats, NGO workers, business travellers and so on, who might face very different issues than someone just coming to soak up the local culture.

Make sure you take in all the safety information, as having knowledge is vital. Do turn the volume knob on that information down from about 10 to about a 6: read enough to make you avoid that questionable neighbourhood, but not so much that you're travelling with constant cold sweats.

Basic ways to stay safe

The following points may strike you as common sense, and they are. Travel safety advice often boils down to acting in responsible and sensible ways...

- **Ask locals about safety.** No one knows better than the people who live there. For instance, ask the receptionist at your hostel or hotel. Typically, you will be told that it's all fine, though sometimes you will be given a vital tip about not venturing into a particular rough area.

- **Get safety information from a guidebook.** This will also help you avoid any particularly sketchy areas.
- **Don't divulge information unless truly necessary.** That random person you just met doesn't really have to know what hotel or hostel you are staying. You don't have to tell people details that you don't want to share.
- **Don't follow a stranger somewhere (unless you actually trust them)** Anyone trying to get you to follow them somewhere should be treated with suspicion. Okay, so maybe not your tour guide—he's legit. But if a stranger spontaneously singles you out and bends over backwards to try to isolate you, you may be dealing with a scammer (or worse).
- **Take taxis at night.** While this is a good idea in general, it's particularly advisable in cities in developing countries where you might not want to walk the streets at night (unless you know the area is safe). Take official taxis only.
- **Don't get drunk.** Don't go overboard with alcohol, and don't walk home alone drunk while playing with your expensive smartphone (take a taxi).
- **Have a plan when arriving at night.** When you arrive somewhere at night, know where are going. Have a place booked or an address to go to so that you are not needlessly roaming the streets at night with your backpack.
- **Trust your instincts.** Our puny human brains actually seem pretty good at intuitively judging whether things are OK or not. If a situation doesn't feel right, too good to be true, or just plain weird, bail. Never feel bad about bailing from a situation you're not comfortable with.

Why you shouldn't rely solely on the news

Travel advisories and locals with deep knowledge of a particular area are useful sources for safety information. The news on the other hand can be a much less useful indicator for overall safety.

What we hear about faraway places tends to be only the bad news, as "not much happened here, all is fine today" doesn't make for a very juicy story. Bad Things, of course, happen everywhere. Chances are bad things happen from time to time where you live right now, and through selective reading of your local newspaper you could spook yourself just as easily. But of course you know better, because it's easier to put things into perspective when you know a place first-hand.

News is also often about extreme individual incidents, not about broader trends, making it often a poor indicator for travel safety overall. As they say, "follow the trendlines, not the headlines".

If you live in the United States, you might get a particularly skewed impression of other countries. Research has shown that US news media spends some of the least time on foreign news, and when foreign news is covered it is almost always the most extreme and scary stuff (e.g. terrorism in the Middle East). Fear sells: 24/7 cable news in particular relies on loud, scary and sensationalist news to keep people tuning in. The same effect can also be seen in the news media in other countries.

When I told some less-informed Americans in Cancún that not only was I not staying in a resort, but that I would be travelling *through* Mexico, their jaws dropped. All they knew about Mexico was that it was supposedly full of drug lords, gangsters and kidnappers. If only they knew what a wonderful country it is to visit and how, apart from a couple of specific trouble-spots, it's perfectly fine for a tourist to travel through. (That is not saying anything about the locals though, who do often have to live with a lot of nasty stuff. It's always different when you're just a visitor.)

Travelling as a woman

Anyone who thinks there aren't differences between travelling as a man or as a woman surely suffers from a lack of imagination. Unfortunately, there *are* some differences, especially in the realm of personal safety. Not only do women have to consider all the usual safety issues, there's also the possibility of harassment or even sexual assault, which add an often unspoken dimension to any safety considerations.

The advice given to female travellers typically isn't that different from the advice given in general however. E.g. do your research, watch your stuff, be aware of your surroundings and avoid, say, walking around alone at night in sketchy areas. Some female travellers advocate specific safety measures such as bringing a safety whistle, or a doorstop that can be used to prevent people from entering your room at night.

Apart from any safety issues, female travellers may also have to grapple with cultural issues as there are hugely varying degrees of gender equality around the world.

Macho behaviour and catcalling is common in Latin America and some Mediterranean countries for example, though I have been told is not necessarily threatening but can be irritating and inappropriate. In some countries men will give foreign women excessive levels of attention unless you say you're married or that your husband will be joining you in a few days. Some female travellers recommend wearing a wedding ring for this purpose even if you aren't actually married. (I have yet to meet a traveller who has done this, but it seems like a good trick.)

One common piece of advice is to dress appropriately, i.e. not wearing anything too revealing in cultures where this is not accepted. Wearing a head scarf in Morocco or a longyi in Burma for example will not only prevent unwanted attention but will gain much goodwill with locals in general. While you might find the idea of having to "cover up" offensive, the way of life is simply different in other parts of the world, and so visitors are expected to adapt. Wearing a short skirt or even short sleeves (revealing the shoulders) can provoke strong reactions in some cultures where this is an uncommon sight.

It should be said that women are travelling (solo or otherwise) all over the world all the time, and most countries are safe to visit for women and men alike. While there are definitely some additional challenges for female travellers, they should not stand in the way of travelling anywhere. It is, however, wise to see if there are any specific issues for women travellers in the countries you plan to visit. (The Middle East in particular can be more difficult for women.)

The following articles are well worth reading for some personal views on the subject from experienced female travellers. They can provide some great anecdotes that yours truly (a male traveller) cannot:

www.adventurouskate.com/never-compromise-your-travel-ideals

www.adventurouskate.com/why-you-no-have-boyfriend

www.nomadicmatt.com/travel-blogs/solo-female-travel-differences

www.hostelworld.com/blog/solo-female-travel-nine-myths-and-one-truth/155970

Dealing with worried parents

Much of the e-mail I receive about travel safety doesn't actually come from travellers, but from their mothers.

"My son has advised me he is leaving for Asia", a recent one began. "I just want to cry all the time. I'm so worried."

Another mother writes: "I'm basically scared out of my mind. I want to support my daughter, but I don't think it's responsible for her to do this right now. Am I crazy? I'm hoping you can tell me some good news so I'm able to sleep."

Oof...

If you are a younger or perhaps first-time traveller, remember to be sensitive to the feelings of any parents or other loved ones. This could be a really big deal to them. And they might look at things a little differently from the way you look at them.

Of course, their fears might well be overblown. Perhaps it's because they were born in a different time: some countries that used to be dangerous no longer are. Maybe your parents have never travelled themselves, or maybe there's just a generational gap. When people travelled back in the day, their only means of communication were hugely expensive international landline calls and maybe the odd postcard. Travelling in those days was much scarier than it is today; now you can easily Skype, e-mail or text message with anyone almost anywhere, and thanks to the internet you are never without vital information.

But maybe your parents have reasonable concerns regarding your safety. Consider if, in fact, they might have a point. Can you deal with the practical challenges of travel? Are you one to naively walk into a situation that could potentially be dangerous? Have you gotten in trouble before? Perhaps you legitimately lack the life experience to tackle the journey you are planning right now. There's no shame in going to easier countries first, where you can level up your travel and life skills before truly going in deep.

If you want to get sceptical parents on board, it helps to share information. Share with them links of the things you've read on the internet. Show them that extensively dog-eared and footnoted travel guide. Run them through all the steps you have taken to prepare yourself for your trip, and allow them to participate in your research to a degree so they can gain confidence in the same way that you are doing. The more diligent and informed you seem, the more your parents might be persuaded that you are not just being impulsive and irrational but that you've got this thing under control.

Offer to keep parents in the loop during your journey, for instance by sending a quick text message or e-mail updating them about your location every time you check into a different hotel. I'm 32 and I still do this for my parents all the time, and they keep telling me this makes their lives so much better when I'm out there somewhere.

Precautions against theft

Backpackers can be tempting targets for thieves, particularly in lower-income countries where they may be seen as very rich by local standards. Fortunately, most theft is purely opportunistic, so by taking some basic precautions you can greatly minimize the chances of having anything stolen.

Secure your belongings at your place of accommodation

Important possessions are kept safest either on your body (for instance, in a travel pouch hidden underneath your clothes) or secured at your place of accommodation.

Hostels and guesthouses often provide lockers for your valuables, and hotels often have safes. If you have a private room, your stuff is reasonably safe behind a locked door. Hostels and hotels will usually have a reputation to uphold, especially if they are reviewed on the internet, and while they may not assume responsibility for any theft they generally do their best to prevent it. Most hotels and hostels have 24/7 staff on site.

Be mindful when in transit

Belongings are most vulnerable when you are moving around, so always keep an eye on your bags, especially if you have just arrived somewhere new and you are still orientating yourself. If you really have to leave your bags out of sight for a moment, ask your travel partner or someone you trust to keep an eye on it.

Don't keep things in an easily pick-pocketable place, such as your back pockets or readily accessible back compartments in your bag.

Be especially careful with storing bags in overhead compartments in buses or trains as someone could swipe your belongings while you are asleep. One way to make this more difficult is to use a retractable wire lock to chain your bag around a bar or pole. Another way is to travel with a bag that is small enough to place next to you or underneath your chair.

Hide your most important stuff

Put things like money, bank cards and passports in secret hiding places. Many backpacks have a secret compartment where you can keep such important items. Some travellers like to use a money pouch, which you can keep under your clothes. There are also various gadgets on the market with hidden compartments, including belts, hats and even underwear. ("Hmm, is that a passport in your boxers, or are you just happy to see me?")

Don't show off your bling

Another way to avoid theft is to not make yourself look like a high-value target. Leave watches, expensive jewellery or anything else that says "I'm rich, pick me!" at home. You can also try to make valuable items (such as electronics) appear less valuable. For instance, a trick used by some photographers is to put ugly brown tape and elastic bands around their SLRs, making it look like the camera is barely holding together even though it may be brand new.

Consider not bringing valuables

Ultimately the best way not to lose something is not to bring it in the first place. For instance, instead of an expensive smartphone you could bring a $5 to $10 burner phone that you won't mind losing so much. While these may be ancient in design, they will keep going on a single battery charge for up to 30 days. You will quickly find that, thanks to e-mail and Skype, you do a lot less texting and calling while you are away anyway.

Use apps to track your electronics

If you are bringing a smartphone, laptop or tablet, have it set up so that you can trace the device if it gets lost or stolen. Apple provides an app called Find my iPhone. On Android there are third party apps such as Where's My Droid, Seekdroid Lite, and AntiDroidTheft. You may also want to look at an app called Prey which works for smartphones as well as laptops (www.preyproject.com).

Have backups of important items and documents

Finally, you will be better prepared for the unlikely event of theft by having duplicates of important documents and items (either as backups or to make replacing the originals easier) and ensuring key information will still be available to you.

Make sure you have multiple means of payment. For instance, bring both a bank and a credit card, and keep them separate.

Finally, collect all your important information. Write down emergency contact numbers, the details of your travel insurance (the insurer details, your policy number, and the phone numbers of their 24-hour helplines) and details of your bank account(s) along with your bank's 24-hour helpline number in case your card gets stolen. You can make copies of these details, either as physical print-outs or as digital files that you can access easily.

What if your bank card gets stolen?

In the unlikely event (there's that little phrase again...) that your bank card gets lost or stolen, don't panic just yet. While this is certainly not fun, you won't be entirely helpless in this situation.

The first thing you should do is call your bank immediately to let them know your card is lost, so that they can block it. Banks always have a 24/7 helpline specifically for reporting loss or theft.

Next, see if you can get your bank to get you a replacement card. It may well be possible to have a replacement sent to where you currently are, though this can take a week or two, which won't help you out straight away.

In the short term, use any emergency cash you might have. Beyond this, Western Union can be a real saviour, as this money transfer service has locations all over the world. You will have to send money to Western Union by wire, which you can then pick up in cash at a Western Union affiliated shop, post office, or bank. If you still have access to your internet banking, or if you can give your bank instructions by phone, then you can set up a Western Union transfer yourself. Otherwise, you may have to rely on your family to transfer money to Western Union for you to pick up.

I once lost my two bank cards (they weren't stolen, but they both got blocked for different reasons). This was not a fun situation, but I still managed to finish the last two months of my trip just by using cash collections from Western Union branches.

Staying safe during activities

Besides crime, there are some other areas of safety. And these are ones that are arguably more important, as they are realistically more likely to affect travellers.

Zip-lining, scuba diving, rafting, etc.

Health and safety regulations can be quite extreme in the West. Sometimes it feels as though the authorities would want to literally put us all in protective bubbles.

In less developed economies, expect health and safety rules to be on the opposite side of the spectrum... in that sometimes there are none. The idea of 'safety first' just hasn't been institutionalized everywhere around the world. So if you are going to participate in any sports or activities, it's worth checking the reviews online. Always expect a safety briefing and don't trust shoddy equipment.

Of course, usually things will be just fine. A quick look at a site like TripAdvisor is usually sufficient to get a good idea of a company's reputation.

If you are going to Scuba dive, as many people do when travelling in tropical destinations, look for dive shops that are officially affiliated with international organizations such as PADI and SSI. These organisations maintain strong worldwide standards, and periodically evaluate dive shops on a wide range of criteria. Other sports have similar international organisations and accreditations.

Traffic safety

Many countries are lax when it comes to traffic rules and regulations. For instance, in Thailand it is perfectly possible to rent a motorbike without a license, and in practice wearing a helmet is entirely optional.

Although I had never ridden a motorbike before, I jumped at the opportunity to rent one in Thailand in the town of Pai, as it was simply the best way to get around the area. It took a few moments to figure things out, but before I knew it I was riding through beautiful landscapes with my head in the wind and a big grin on my face. Sometimes I was accompanied by Rambo, a dog from the hostel that would hitch rides into town by sitting on the floorboard. Good times.

Puttering around a sleepy town or riding through quiet country roads is probably not a huge issue, even without prior experience. On the other hand, there are plenty of foreigners blasting around Thailand at hyper speeds of over 80 km/h, even without a helmet or any protective gear. This is... less wise. City traffic can also be extremely chaotic and difficult to deal with if you're not accustomed to the local style of driving.

Throughout South-East Asia I've met travellers with bandages from motorbike accidents. Getting scars or wounds from accidents is even euphemistically referred to in Thailand as "getting a Thai tattoo", and in Indonesia they're called a "Bali kiss". That there's names for it at all suggests how common accidents are. The names are cute but hide the fact that some injuries are serious, and that there are record fatalities each year.

Be careful, and even if you are a responsible driver, it's good to keep in mind that locals don't always stick to traffic rules.

Worldwide, the most traffic deaths occur in Middle Eastern and African countries, with Asian and Latin American countries not far behind. Countries like Myanmar, Thailand, Malaysia, Venezuela, Peru, Mexico and the

Philippines (just to name a few) score particularly badly in the UN's annual road safety rankings, so if you do decide to drive or ride a motorcycle, be extra careful.

Alcohol or drugs

Alcohol is cheap in places, even sold by the bucket load. That can be cause for a big night out (and a big hangover the next day). Keep your head screwed on though as people tend to do stupid things when drunk. Be wary in particular of wandering drunk around at night and take taxis home if needed.

Drugs may be readily available in certain parts of the world and even sold openly sometimes (for instance, magic mushrooms are sold in some bars in Asia). But while drugs can appear to be tolerated in some parts, possession is usually still illegal, and police may not be quite as understanding as you would hope or expect. Drugs charges are sometimes used for collecting bribes from foreigners, and there have even been reports of entrapment (for instance at the infamous Full Moon Party in Thailand, where dealers are often in cahoots with the police).

When dealers sell drugs to foreign travellers, they also have little incentive to provide good product as return customers are rare. One cautionary tale comes from a guy I met in Thailand who bought what he thought was MDMA, but whatever it actually was, it had no effect on him other than to make him sick like a dog for days. The dealer was of course nowhere to be found.

It might also not be the best idea to experiment with drugs in a very unfamiliar environment or with people you might not know very well. This is particularly true about hallucinogenics.

Anything said about drugs will surely come across as either patronizing to some, or as seemingly condoning drugs to others, so the topic will always be controversial. Perhaps the best thing to say about drugs is to be very careful as there are various risks involved. Better yet, of course, is to keep your travels drug-free.

Hiking safety

Hiking independently can be difficult in some low-income countries, as trails are not always marked and hiking maps not always available. Presumably many local authorities avoid setting up a hiking infrastructure so that travellers are forced to hire private guides. Either make sure you know there is a good route to follow, or get a guide to show you the way.

You may be used to hiking alone at home in areas you know well, but this would be a bad idea in unfamiliar territory abroad. As a rule of thumb, don't hike alone (aside from maybe very short or very well-marked trails). You could get into a lot of trouble if you get lost or get injured.

If you are hiking without a guide, let someone know where you are going. This can be the staff at your last hostel, or if you are visiting a national park you could check in at the entrance.

If you ever get lost, first try to back-track. Never split up a group to go in different directions: it is always better to stick together. If you are completely and utterly lost, try to find a river, and follow it downstream.

Finally, make sure you bring some rain cover, food and especially plenty of water with you.

Avoiding scams and confidence tricks

You may on your travels encounter the occasional scammer or trickster, particularly in countries where there is a big income disparity between locals and foreigners. Most scams are simply ways to deceive or coerce you into paying money.

One famous scam involves claiming you have damaged a rented motorbike or other equipment when clearly you have not. They will point to what is clearly a 'pre-existing condition', though you will be demanded enormous charges for repair. Sometimes the police are in cahoots with these scammers, offering to mediate towards a lower settlement but actually getting a slice of the pie.

Another common scam is the dual menu switch-a-roo in bars and restaurants, where one menu with reasonable prices is swapped for another one with exorbitant ones. You will still be expected to pay the bill. If you refuse, the waiter may get aggressive or threaten to call the police.

If you travel for any significant length of time you will probably encounter a scam or two. While you may not avoid them entirely, you can be better prepared for them by reading up on common scams in your guidebook or on Wikivoyage. Most scams are relatively innocent, though there are a few more nefarious ones out there which may result in outright theft or intimidation.

A few good precautions against getting tricked:

- Always take photos or a video of any vehicles or equipment you intend to rent.
- Check currency exchange rates to ensure you are not being overcharged by a money exchanger.
- Be wary of any stranger who seems to be singling you out very specifically and giving you extended special attention, especially if they are trying to persuade you to follow them anywhere. Don't share information about where you are staying if it's not any of their business.
- Don't feel as though you have to forever stay polite and reasonable just because someone is friendly or polite towards you. Scammers know that most people will avoid confrontation, so they will just keep trying and trying. Don't feel bad about utterly ignoring someone or firmly telling them off.
- Be firm with cab drivers. They are the grand masters of overcharging, tampering with meters, and so on. They will also often claim a hotel or attraction you want to go to is closed / too expensive / full / under renovation / eaten by a monster, but they *just* so happen to know the perfect alternative, which is a dodgy place that they earn commission off. It may sound harsh, but be somewhat suspicious of cab drivers by default.

Some scammers will have no qualms preying on people's goodwill even in the most unethical ways. In Vietnam I was repeatedly approached by someone claiming to be a representative of the Red Cross collecting money for the disabled. (Vietnam still has many disabled people from the war and from land mines.) She had an official-looking badge and was trying to sell toothpicks in exchange for donations. This struck me as rather bizarre, though I chalked it down to some kind of cultural misunderstanding—perhaps toothpicks were somehow symbolic in Vietnam?

When she got out a little booklet showing handwritten names of donors along with their hefty donations ($15, $40, etc.) alarm bells went off in my head. Surely this is scam territory: she was clearly priming me for making a large donation, which probably isn't the sort of tactic the Red Cross would use. Or did she just innocently write down the names of particularly generous people, as her personal high score list? Maybe I was just being paranoid? After her continued pleading I ended up giving her a bunch of money. Perhaps I was just sick of having to deal with the situation.

Even though I was briefly on to the whole charade I had buckled. It was only minutes later that I was kicking myself for it. As I soon found out, the whole thing is in fact a confirmed scam. The Red Cross badge is a fake, but it flies by so quickly you don't have a chance to notice.

If you do get stung, don't be too hard on yourself. You were simply deceived, and your trust or generosity were taken advantage of. Just chalk it up to experience and try to avoid such a situation next time.

Needless to say, you shouldn't turn aggressive towards scammers, as this could have unwanted consequences. While scams are frustrating, it is not worth endangering your personal safety over some money, even if it's out of principle.

Digital security and backups

As careful as people usually are with their physical belongings, many forget to apply the same care to their digital files as well as their internet connections. This is unfortunate as constantly using different computers or different Wi-Fi signals poses increased risks compared to only using your computer at home.

Fortunately, you don't need to be a computer expert to ensure your data and login details are much safer.

Using public computers

Many travellers regularly use public computers, such as those at hostels or internet cafes. Sadly, these are not very secure, nor are they always convenient to use.

While most internet cafes completely wipe and reinstall their computers every so often, they still tend to be festering hives of malware, viruses and dubious plug-in apps. Programs called key-loggers can also relay all keyboard input (including credit card numbers) to a third party, even unbeknownst to the computer's owner. It's therefore best not to submit private data or credit card information on a public computer, if at all possible.

To add an additional layer of security to your internet use you can use LastPass (www.lastpass.com) or 1Password (www.agilebits.com). These browser plug-ins store your passwords on a server using advanced encryption. You will only need to remember one master password, and it will fill out all the other ones (Facebook, email, etc.) automatically while you are logged in. LastPass also has a password input console that allows you to enter a password with the mouse instead of the keyboard, making it completely safe from keyloggers.

Using public Wi-Fi on your own device

Your connection is not completely 100% secure on a public Wi-Fi, even if you've had to fill in a password to connect, though it takes a dedicated hacker to steal information like credit card numbers. Generally, when you are using Wi-Fi on your own device (laptop, tablet or smartphone) it is reasonably secure.

However, make sure the devices themselves are secure as well. Put a password on it, and make sure the device goes to the lock screen after a certain period of inactivity.

Consider installing an anti-theft solution on your devices. A popular one is Prey, which works on Windows, Mac, Android and iOS. It lets you track a stolen device, even take a photo of the thief using the webcam, and you can use it to remotely wipe all your passwords and sensitive information. It is free for one device, or $5 per month for up to 3 devices. (www.preyproject.com)

Keeping backups

Make backups of your important files, especially photos, as these will be lost forever if your camera were to get stolen. Making backups is a *really* simple precaution and yet **lots** of people forget to do this and end up crying about it later. Physical stuff can always be replaced in an emergency (again, in the unlikely event...), but losing all your photos, videos, memories, and other digital files is a real disaster as you will never be able to get them back.

Since internet connections are often very slow in remote locations, it's best to take a two-step approach to backups. First make a copy of your files onto another SD card, USB stick, portable USB drive or laptop harddrive. Then when you are in a city with fast internet, upload the backup to an online service, or use a cloud storage service to have this done automatically.

Popular cloud storage services include Dropbox, Google Drive, Google Picasaweb (for photos), Microsoft's OneDrive, and Apple's iCloud.

Key points from this chapter

- The world is, by and large, quite safe. **Don't rely exclusively on the news** to inform you about the safety in different countries, as it can easily give you a skewed perspective.
- That said, it's also **important not to be naive**. As with many other things, travel does carry some risk, and so you don't want to walk into situations blind.
- Apply all the **common sense precautions** and **protect your belongings** from possible theft.
- Most countries are fine to visit, though you can hugely reduce the risk of encountering any issues by avoiding any known trouble spots (such as areas with high crime). **Read safety advisories** and ask about the local situation.

- Read up on **known scams** as well.
- While most people only think of axe murderers as potential safety issues, in reality any **safety issues around hiking and other activities or traffic safety**, are much more likely to affect a traveller.
- Be sure to keep in mind digital security as well. **Always make backups of any important files.**

[9]

Travel health

THIS CHAPTER WILL GO INTO some important travel health issues, but don't let words like "malaria" or "dengue" give you too much heebie-jeebies. There are only a handful of major health dangers that directly affect travellers, and so long as you are responsible and take appropriate preventative measures, there is not too much to worry about.

There are two steps you should always take before your departure:

1. **Buy travel insurance with comprehensive medical coverage**. This is simply a good precaution, and discussed in more detail earlier in chapter 7.

2. **Visit your doctor and inform them of your travel plans.** Do this well in advance; 6 to 8 weeks before planned departure is generally recommended, as this will give sufficient time for any vaccinations that you potentially need to take effect. It will also provide enough time to test which type of malaria tablets are best suited to you, assuming any malaria prophylaxis is recommended to you for your intended destinations.

Make sure you are informed about the main health issues out there, which we will briefly cover in a moment, and be sure to get any vaccinations that are specifically recommended to you by your doctor.

Before we go ahead it's necessary for me to offer a slight disclaimer, as the information provided in this chapter is for general travel health advice only. Key health details are sourced from the UK's National Health Service and the

World Health Organization, as well as from personal travel experiences, though this is not a replacement for a personal consultation with your travel health advisor.

Getting your vaccinations

If you are travelling to a Western country you may not need any particular vaccinations at all, as many diseases do not commonly occur here. If you are going to Africa, Asia or South America the need for vaccinations becomes much more likely.

Whether your doctor will advise you to take specific vaccinations depends largely on where you are planning to travel, as some diseases are only prevalent in some regions. For this reason, be sure to give your doctor a complete run-down of your travel plans.

You should also tell your doctor if you expect to be in any sort of unusual circumstance beyond just ordinary travel—say, volunteering in slum or refugee areas, or spending lots of time in paddy fields during monsoon season— as this could affect what kind of preventative measures you need.

Some vaccinations are extremely routine and you will have usually had these as a child, such as for measles, polio or meningitis C. If you are already insured under a health program these vaccinations are most likely free of charge, so nothing should stop you from getting them, if for some reason you haven't had them already.

There are a couple of other diseases that are specifically relevant to travellers (most of which have vaccinations available):

Typhoid Fever

An infection caused by bacteria, spread by way of contaminated food or water in areas of poor sanitation. A vaccination will protect you completely for up to 3 years and is standard for travellers.

Hepatitis A

A disease spread by way of contaminated food or water. This is also a standard vaccination for travellers. Once fully vaccinated you will be immune for up to 20 years.

Hepatitis B

Spread primarily through unprotected sex, or sometimes through needles that were not properly sterilized (e.g. tattoo needles). Not a routine vaccination for travellers, though it is possible you will be provided one in combination with either Hepatitis A or Typhoid.

Yellow Fever

Yellow Fever is spread by mosquitos and is fatal in about 10% of cases. A vaccination will protect you completely for at least 10 years. You should get a Yellow Fever vaccination if you are going to Latin America or Sub-Saharan Africa, but not if you are going to Asia (or elsewhere) as the disease does not occur there.

You may need proof of Yellow Fever vaccination to enter some countries in Latin America or Africa. Be sure to get vaccinated and to get the accompanying certification from your doctor (typically a small booklet that you can staple into your passport).

Rabies

Rabies is a disease transmitted from animals to humans, most often through a bite from an infected dog. A vaccine is not routinely given to travellers, but may still be recommended if you are particularly at risk in some way, for example if you will be trekking extensively in areas where rabies occurs or if you are going to regions where there is no access to prompt medical care.

A rabies shot is relatively expensive: it costs between £120 and £150 in the UK (about $225) and this is perhaps one reason not everyone chooses to get it. The vaccination also does not make you immune: it merely buys you some additional time in the unlikely event that you get rabies and cannot receive medical attention within a few days (for instance, if you are in a very remote part of the world). Most travellers go without a rabies shot, though it's possible that your specific travel plans do warrant one.

Dengue Fever

Dengue is an increasingly common infection that knows, at this time, no vaccination or cure. It is a tropical disease most common in Asia, sub-Saharan Africa, and Latin America and is spread by mosquitoes that bite during the day (as opposed to malaria, which is spread by another type of mosquito that bites between dusk and dawn). Symptoms include high fever, headache, pain behind the eyes, and bone, muscle and joint pain.

Fortunately, it is not life threatening and usually clears up by itself within around one to two weeks, provided you rest properly (you might potentially have to recover in a hospital). It is however an extremely painful disease and in no way a pleasant experience to go through. While rare, dengue fever is another good reason to avoid mosquito bites; use mosquito repellent and sleep under mosquito nets where necessary.

Malaria protection

Finally, there is malaria—surely the most talked about health issue for travellers.

Malaria is, first of all, a serious disease. It can sometimes be fatal if it is not diagnosed and treated promptly. Symptoms include fever, vomiting, sweats and chills, muscle pains, headaches and diarrhoea. These symptoms develop some time after being bitten by an infected mosquito—anywhere ranging from 7 days to up to a year after infection.

However, you should also understand that so long as malaria is diagnosed and treated promptly, virtually everyone will make a full recovery. While there is currently no vaccine, anti-malarial medication does exist and can be used both to prevent and treat malaria. This, in addition to using common methods for avoiding mosquito bites, can help protect you against malaria (though no method is 100% effective).

Malaria can be highly endemic in some areas and barely existent or non-existent in others. Africa remains the most problematic, with high-risk areas across the continent. The main exceptions in Africa, where there is actually a very low risk, are any of the countries above the Sahara Desert (e.g. Egypt. Morocco, Tunisia) as well as the countries in the very south (including South Africa, Botswana and Namibia). West, Central and East Africa are, broadly speaking, regions where increased caution is advised. Your doctor will probably recommend you take malaria prophylaxis before going to these parts.

Outside of Africa, the threat is dramatically less severe. Areas that remain high risk are typically found in the more remote parts of the world, including the jungles of Papua New Guinea, Borneo, and the depths of the Amazon. Parts of Southeast Asia also have a low-to-moderate malaria risk.

Much effort has been made in combating the disease over the past years and decades. Speaking of Southeast Asia, much of Thailand and The Philippines, for instance, is malaria free. Aside from a few isolated pockets, Central America is a low risk area. India sees relatively few cases, and some countries in South America have officially eradicated the disease.

If you want to know exactly where malaria occurs, consult the malaria maps offered by the World Health Organization as these are the most reliable and up-to-date. You can find these at:

http://www.who.int/malaria/publications/country-profiles/

Click the country you want to know about and your browser will open a PDF with all sorts of information. Most of the details aren't relevant to travellers, but the key thing to look for is the map at the top. White areas on this map have no malaria, while red areas are the most high-risk. You might find that the current situation is quite different from how it's depicted in, for instance, older guidebooks from a few years ago. For instance, while some old maps display Brazil entirely in red (i.e. 'high threat'), the vast majority of the country is in fact malaria-free.

Be sure to consult your general practitioner or travel health advisor at least 6 to 8 weeks before your trip. If anti-malarial tablets are recommended to you, they may want you to try them out first as they all have different side-effects that affect some people more than others (so your doctor will want to find the right one for you).

While anti-malaria tablets are one line of possible defence, another is to avoid mosquito bites in the first place. Good preventative measures include:

- Using mosquito repellent containing DEET. The concentration of DEET varies per product. Around 50% is considered extremely strong, while somewhere up to 30% is more common.
- Keeping windows in your room closed if there is no mosquito gauze in the window frame.
- Sleeping under a mosquito net where necessary. If you are going to sub-Saharan Africa, bringing your own net may be advisable.

- If your room has a fan or air conditioning unit, use it. Mosquitos don't like the wind or low temperatures.

If you get fever or other symptoms after having been in any malarial area, be sure to tell your doctor as this will allow them to investigate rather than assume it's just a common fever.

Other health issues or annoyances

Rest assured, we have now covered the serious diseases you need to know about. The following are a few other common health issues or annoyances which, while not as serious as infectious diseases, are still good to be aware of.

Altitude sickness

As a rough rule of thumb, you can get affected by altitude effects if you are anywhere over 2,400m above sea level. These effects can range from simply being out of breath often, to more severe effects such as persistent headaches or feeling sick to your stomach.

One way to experience the effects of altitude change in a dramatic way is to fly straight from Lima in Peru (elevation: sea level) to Cusco (elevation: 3,399 m), as I once did. After landing, you and everyone else on the plane will walk through the terminal in a surreal slow-motion, as though everyone suddenly and inexplicably became extremely stoned. While my brain kept telling my body to walk faster, it just wouldn't do it. A walk up a few steps could leave me huffing and puffing.

This phenomenon is caused by the thinner air at higher altitudes: because you take in less oxygen with every breath, you will be out of breath faster. If your body has not had any time to adjust, the effects will be particularly noticeable.

If you go to a high altitude, allow yourself some time to acclimatize by taking it easy for a day or two. This will give your body a chance to produce more red blood cells, which help deliver more oxygen to your body tissues. Usually you will begin noticing some improvement after 24 to 48 hours. (Of course, if you have gradually been going higher into the mountains over a period of many days, your body may have already adjusted along the way.)

If you are travelling in the Andes (e.g. Chile, Bolivia, Peru) it is said that chewing coca leaves or drinking coca tea will help with altitude sickness, though this claim has not been tested by science.

Bed bugs

Bed bugs can be an issue on rare occasions. These tiny bugs are only a few millimetres in size and sometimes live under mattresses. They do not carry disease and are rather harmless, though they will bite humans at night—sucking your blood the same way a mosquito would. You will know you have bed bugs if you find little clusters of red marks on your skin in the morning, similar to mosquito bites but smaller and closer together.

You might have to take reports about bed bugs with a pinch of salt, however. Many travellers misidentify mosquito bites as bed bug bites and then write a bad review of a hotel. Others might just have a bad experience with customer service and, in their vindictiveness, suggest a place has bed bugs as well. You have to sympathize with hotel and hostel owners who either have to deal with such false alarms, or who promptly respond to genuine bed bug sightings but still have to live with a negative review for months or years after.

Bed bugs are not necessarily a sign of poor hygiene or carelessness on part of a hotel: they can show up in a luxury hotel just as easily as in a grungy budget hostel. Upmarket hotels in New York City had problems with them in the recent past, as was eagerly reported in the media.

While these little vampires are unpleasant to think about, they are a fairly rare occurrence. All the hype over bed bugs might just be a little overblown, if you ask this author anyway. It might be anecdotal, but after travelling the world for a combined three years, and staying in a different place every couple of days (including some pretty... well, rustic places), I encountered bed bugs only once. I can also count on a single hand the number of people I met that had to deal with them as well. Make of that what you will.

That said, if you do get bed bugs, inform the hotel staff as they will probably want to try and get rid of them. Get another bed in another room, or move to another place. Wash any clothes or fabrics that were in contact with your bed at a high temperature (such as 60° C or 140°F), as this will kill any bugs trying to hitch a ride with you. Just to be thorough, you could wash all of your clothes in this way.

Some hostels request that you do not put any of your bags on your bed, as this is how bed bugs end up travelling from one place to another.

Food safety and hygiene

As a traveller you will surely end up eating different food than at home, and due to constantly being on the move you will probably eat on an irregular schedule as well. As a result, your digestive system may be a little off at times. For instance, you may become a bit constipated or get some minor (non-critical) diarrhoea. This is nothing to worry about as it is simply part of being in a new environment. Most people find that it becomes much less of an issue over time.

That said, if you are visiting developing countries where hygiene standards can be rather poor, you may face more severe diarrhoea at some point. This is what is sometimes referred to as the Traveller's Curse. There are some other creative euphemisms in use depending on the location: people speak of Delhi Belly in India and Montezuma's Revenge in Mexico.

Getting food poisoning is not fun. If you are travelling in developing countries for any significant length of time, it is unfortunately something you may have just to deal with at some point.

The worst situation you could find yourself in is, say, being stuck on a bus without a toilet and feeling like you could be having a severe bowel emergency at any time. For these scenarios it's a good idea to have some imodium pills with you. Imodium (also known by its non-brand name loperamide) has a constipating effect, and while this doesn't address the root cause, it can help you stay out of trouble in the short term.

If you get food poisoning, the best thing you can do is to simply take it easy for a while. Cancel or delay any transit, tours, or activities you had planned. Stay in your room, maybe read a book, and stay within easy reach of a toilet. Drink plenty of water and try to eat when your body feels up to it again. Things usually get better within 24 to 48 hours. You will probably be cursing "FML!" repeatedly during this time, but it should all pass and you should be back on your feet soon.

There are fortunately some things you can do to prevent an upset stomach, or at least significantly reduce the chances:

- **Drink only bottled water.** In many countries there is some risk of tap water being contaminated (at least without boiling it first) and so this is best avoided, though bottled water is almost universally safe to drink.

- **Avoid sketchy-looking food.** If you have the choice between a freshly prepared dish and a fly-covered buffet that clearly has been sitting in the sun all day, the choice is clear. Anything that looks like it isn't fresh or hasn't been handled well probably isn't going to be worth it.

- **Eat where locals eat.** If a food stall has many locals waiting in line, or if a restaurant looks lively with many local customers, that's usually a sign the food will be of a high standard. Places frequented by locals have a reputation to maintain.

- **Wash your hands.** Sounds obvious, but this can be a challenge at times when there is no soap available (this is common in restrooms in developing countries). Have some anti-bacterial gel with you for such situations.

- **Avoid drinks with icecubes.** These are often made with potentially contaminated tap water instead of safe/bottled water. Some restaurants and street vendors along the backpacker trails have gotten the message about this however and will clearly state their ice cubes are safe—in this case there's little reason to doubt them.

- **Take it easy on the spicy food.** If you are not used to spicy food you may want to gradually build up a tolerance instead of jumping straight in, or avoid it entirely if you are particularly sensitive. Spicy food can cause diarrhoea as it tends to irritate the intestines, which the body responds to by releasing more water to dilute the irritant.

Resist the urge to pile on the red chilies if your body is not used to spiciness of such magnitude.

- **Boil it, cook it, peel it or forget it.** This is a common piece of advice for food safety. If it's been cooked/boiled and made to order, it's probably safe. If it's fruit that can be peeled, it's probably safe too.

With all these tips and warnings, you might get the impression that food poisoning is a very regular occurrence. Severe bowel problems are, fortunately, not quite as common as people imagine them to be. You could travel for a whole year and get hit maybe once or twice—which certainly isn't fun but is still quite manageable. Of course, it's also possible you will get unlucky and experience much worse... but for most travellers this doesn't seem to be the case. (Arguably the main exception is India, where tummy problems are definitely par for the course.)

While being a little cautious with food safety is a good idea, being overly paranoid is not, as this could easily make you miss out on many culinary highlights around the world.

Don't be afraid to eat at places like this. (The best chicken broth ever—Penang, Malaysia)

For example, some say you should never eat raw fish in developing countries, but does that mean you should not eat ceviche in Peru, a dish that this country is famous for? I know what my answer is: definitely eat the ceviche. It's absolutely delicious and you don't want to miss it.

Some might never touch any fruit shakes at all out of fear that it may include some tap water, but personally I would say to hell with that and have all the fruit shakes you want. Why should you not have some delicious fruit shakes, especially if they are chuck full of vitamins and cost only a dollar or two?

Similarly, do not be afraid to eat any street food that passes your basic trust tests. It's often at food stalls, food trucks, and little roadside eateries that you can find the really good stuff. Their cooks have often specialized in making the same dish for years or even decades, and they know to do it just right. Eat the street food, unless there is particular reason not to.

Really, don't be afraid to eat from places that seem a little basic; it's all part of the experience. There's nothing like sitting down on a tiny plastic chair on a roadside in Ho Chi Minh City and getting yourself a nice bowl of steaming hot pho noodles along with all the usual herbs, beansprouts, limes, and chillies that you can add to taste. It's pure happiness.

While you clearly should avoid dodgy food, don't think you should eat in "tourist" restaurants only—in fact, it's sometimes these restaurants where standards may be lax. Apply common sense precautions, but don't let it stop you from sampling the traditional cuisines in the same places that locals get them too.

Getting medical assistance

If you get sick while travelling and it is nothing too severe, simply do as you would at home: rest, take it easy, take appropriate medicine if necessary, and make sure you drink and eat well.

If you require a doctor abroad, unless you are very far removed from civilization it is usually not too difficult to find a general practitioner or clinic nearby. Ask at your hotel reception where you can find one. Communication with doctors is not usually an issue: they tend to be well-educated and so they will often be able to speak some English even in countries where this is not so common in general.

Before you go out to receive medical help, call your travel insurer's 24-hour medical helpline or their claims advice hotline. These are not just for extreme emergencies; making such a call could be a precondition for any claims you make later. It's best to contact your insurer for anything for which the cost might exceed your standard excess. Be sure to keep receipts if you plan to claim anything back from your insurance.

When buying medicine in pharmacies, keep in mind that you may know certain medicine by their brand name rather than their medical name. Nurofen or Advil are brand names for ibuprofen painkillers, and Imodium is a brand name for loperamide (constipation pills). Not every pharmacist is aware of every brand name as these can be different around the world, but if you write down the generic medical name they will almost definitely be able to help you.

Don't be too proud to go to a doctor. If you have persistent flu symptoms for instance, this could indicate malaria or dengue fever. That's not to say you should panic at the first sign of high body temperature (it's probably just a regular flu), but it's wise to visit a doctor if anything doesn't just resolve itself within a reasonable time. When you are enjoying so many freedoms abroad it is easy to get callous, but your health is a serious matter and a check-up is never a bad idea.

Know when to call it off

While unlikely, if you do end up having a serious medical issue abroad, consider whether you should... well, change your travel plans.

Travellers can be stubborn. One cautionary tale comes from a guy I met in Indonesia, who hurt his foot so badly in an accident that he had to get 22 stitches. Aid was given at a local clinic on a small island. But instead of backtracking to a city with a proper hospital and more qualified staff and facilities, this traveller refused to change his plans in any way, and so he stuck around a hostel for two weeks while walking around awkwardly on crutches. When the wound got infected (possibly due to poor sterilization), he had to be evacuated back to Europe for surgery at great expense.

His family was taken by complete surprise as he had failed to mention the whole incident.

If something unforeseen does happen, it may be difficult to admit defeat. It may be disappointing to have to adjust or even abort part of your travel plans, but it's best to get things looked after properly. You can always come back later.

Key points from this chapter

- **Visit your doctor well in advance of your trip** (6 to 8 weeks) to sort out any vaccinations you need.
- If you are going to Sub-Saharan Africa or South America, **get proof of your Yellow Fever vaccination**.
- If you need medical assistance during your trip, call your insurer's medical helpline before going to a doctor or hospital (unless it's extremely urgent of course). Keep any receipts and medical statements that you may need for a claim.
- **Avoid mosquito bites** by using repellent containing DEET.
- **Don't drink tap water** in developing countries (and in many developed countries for that matter, as it may be heavily chlorinated). Use bottled water for drinking.
- Take a **common sense approach to what you eat**, but don't be afraid to try the local food; you can get a stomach bug just as easily from a tourist restaurant as from a street vendor.

[10]

Connecting with people

THE NIGHT WAS full of stars and the air filled with a cool mountain breeze. We were huddled around a campfire, making marshmallows, drinking rum, and telling tales. We were a typically ragtag bunch of travellers: myself, a 40-something couple from New Zealand, a 30-something guy from Germany, and a 20-something girl from Sweden.

We merrily hummed along to some songs the German guy played on his guitar. When he'd finished his last song, he looked around our circle and said, "You know what's so great about travel? It's the people." This was something we could all easily agree with. And so under that beautiful Bolivian night sky, we all clinked our glasses and cheered.

That guy was right: travel is all about the people. The moments that you often end up remembering the most are ones spent with some of those wonderful, interesting, or just plain funny or weird people you meet along the way. Whether it's your travel buddies, other travellers, or locals that you end up spending time with, the shared experiences and cultural exchanges are always a huge part of travel.

This chapter is all about your interactions with other people. It hopes to answer such burning questions as: who should you travel with (and how will you work well as a team)? How can you meet other travellers along the way?

How *do* you meet locals? But above all, how can you deal with all the cultural and language barriers you will surely face on a daily basis? Let's dig in...

Who to travel with

Who you travel with will affect your journey more than anything else. You could be trapped in a terrible thunderstorm for days, but with the right company you can still have a great time even if you are forced to stay inside. Or you might be visiting the most majestic location on Earth, but not enjoy it at all because you are travelling with a curmudgeon.

As travel writer Pico Yver once wrote, "You take an angry man to the Himalayas, he just starts complaining about the food. Nowhere is magical unless you bring the right eyes to it."

This is why it's essential to be on the same wavelength as your travel partner. You have to travel in good company, and be good company to your travel companion(s).

When it comes to big long-term trips, there are two kinds of ideal travel buddies...

The first and obvious ideal travel buddy is someone you know really well, perhaps a close friend or a soulmate, anyone you are comfortable sharing a big journey with entirely from start to finish. You leave home with that person and come back with that person, and any challenges in between are for you to solve as a team.

The second ideal travel buddy is someone you barely know at all, but met incidentally on your travels. Backpackers who meet in transit or in hostels or guesthouses often team up in ad hoc fashion, forming groups or duos based purely on their current travel plans. Such serendipitous travel buddies are great because the pressures on you as a team are much lower. Either you hit it off well and you keep travelling together, or you say goodbye and go your separate ways. Maybe you like each other and would keep travelling together, but hit a juncture where your travel goals diverge—in this case it's not unthinkable for you to still split up.

Doing this with a travel buddy or partner from home would clearly be bitter-sweet at best or a disaster at worst, so when you set off from home with someone you clearly want to stick it out with them the whole way. This means choosing your travel buddy wisely.

If you don't have someone to go with, you can always go on a big journey solo and meet people along the way. This is more common than you might think. Life circumstances allowing long-term travel are relatively rare, so while many people will go on shorter holidays together, many long-term travellers are on their own. (This chapter touches on solo travel a little bit, though the next chapter goes into more detail on how to travel in this way.)

If you are planning to travel with your partner, make sure your relationship is at a level where it can withstand the potential adversities and frustrations of travel. Successful travel companions approach problems with humour, give each other moral support, and share in the decision-making by communicating well. Inevitably some things on your journey will not go entirely as you had hoped however, and then ideally you want to be able to let out some steam without this immediately undermining your relationship.

Travelling together can be as serious as moving in together. If you plan to travel as a couple and have not done so before, it may be wise to test the waters with a shorter holiday first. You might be totally amazing as a couple at home but struggle under the pressures of being together 24/7, day in, day out. A big journey can either do wonders for your relationship (thanks to so many shared experiences) or it can seriously test it.

If you are planning to travel with a friend, make sure your travel goals and personalities are compatible, and be honest when things are bothering you. If you are not already very close friends, try to get to a place where you can be very open in your communication. You are going to be with each other for quite a while, so you have to be able to operate on that level.

Arguably the most challenging for a long-term trip is to travel as a group. That is to say, a group you formed at home and not an ad hoc one that emerged spontaneously on the trail. As a group you are likely to have broader-ranging needs and goals, which can lead to more compromise and potentially frustration over time. Groups often do well on relatively shorter trips with clearly defined goals, as together it's easy to remain in high spirits and fun to bond over a shared pursuit. But groups can struggle or even fracture when travelling for many months on end, as people's different priorities begin to create tensions. Everything that's said about choosing the right travel partner goes doubly so for a group.

Embracing the backpacker culture

Generally speaking, things work a little differently socially when backpacking than they do at home.

Before I embarked on my first big backpacking trip, I could never have imagined that I would meet hundreds of other travellers on my journey, and even make some lasting friends along the way. I also couldn't have predicted that I would share large parts of my journey with people I encountered randomly. Whether you are travelling solo or together, travel puts you in a different frame of mind that makes it easier to meet people.

After I had spent eight months on my first backpacking trip and had arrived back home in London, it truly hit me how different things can be on the trail. As I looked around the all-too-familiar London Overground train, I noticed that every passenger was either fixated on their phone or staring at the ceiling. This used to be normal to me, but had just become very strange. When a voice on the speakers announced a 15-minute delay to our arrival, it triggered a lovely murmur of British harrumphing around the car. "…Typical" the man next to me said under his breath.

It occurred to me then that I probably wouldn't talk to that man. Nor would I introduce myself to the girl sitting opposite of me reading the Metro newspaper, nor strike up a conversation with the commuter sitting next to her.

But suppose I had found myself in an incredibly spontaneous mood and got into a pleasant conversation with any of these strangers… Would I then suggest we go visit a castle together or travel to Birmingham tomorrow? Would I ask where exactly they will be sleeping tonight, or if they are hungry and would like to join me for food later?

It was only because I had just been backpacking that I as amused by these thoughts, sitting in that dreadfully boring train. I could recall some train rides on my journey that were in every way the polar opposite experience, simply by virtue of there being a couple of strangers with similar goals and mind-set heading the same way.

If you are travelling anywhere on a known traveller's circuit, chances are you will quickly spot some fellow souls on your bus, train or ferry. They probably won't be looking at their phones or newspaper. Chances are they are in a happy mood, and chances are they will want to hear about where you have been and where you are going. Before you know it names will have been exchanged, snacks are being shared, and travel stories are flowing.

Going on a backpacking trip can be like stepping through a mirror into another world. You will find yourself in a place where social interactions work differently and where you can meet people seemingly at every turn. Strangers become acquaintances, even friends, much faster than they normally would.

If you are hitting it off with people you meet on the trail, don't be surprised if people invite you along to things (and it won't be weird for you to extend an invitation to them). This is just how many travellers roll. Not only is this a fun way to travel, but it can also make it easier and reduce costs, for instance by sharing the cost of a cab ride or a tour guide among more people. If you meet people while in transit and they ask you if you have already booked something at the destination, that doesn't mean they are trying to stalk you; they are probably just going to suggest looking for accommodation together, or are simply curious to know where you'll be staying as you might bump into each other again.

While you don't necessarily have to take such a free-wheeling approach to meeting other travellers, you should know that you can team up with other people if the right situation arises.

Sometimes it can feel as though you are all part of one big travelling community, particularly in well-travelled countries. Ad hoc groups can organically form and disband depending on people's individual plans. This is great news if you are travelling solo. If you're travelling as a couple, joining groups can keep you from relying exclusively on each other for the whole duration of the trip. You may love each other dearly, but spend entire days on end with only each other as company and even the best couple can get agitated. Opening yourself up to other travellers (as well as friendly locals) helps to mix things up.

Of course, travel is not always all that sociable, and a lot depends on where you are going. You won't encounter people literally everywhere; some countries or regions are just a bit too far off the map. And sometimes you may simply be going your own way and focusing on your own adventure.

Back home I usually don't want to impose on people, or accept an invitation too eagerly if it's from people I don't really know. I worry less about this when I am backpacking, though it is something I had to learn.

At the start of my very first trip several years ago, I connected with three other travellers at my hostel: a brother and sister from Australia and a girl from the UK. We would often chat over breakfast and eventually took a day-tour together. At one point we discussed our next destination, which happened to be the same for all of us.

The brother mentioned multiple times which hostel they had booked there, but it was too early for me to recognize this was really him saying, "hey, if you'd like to join us that's cool, this is where we are staying". Not yet knowing the backpacker ways, I had booked a different hostel that happened to be on the opposite side of town. I suppose I didn't want to impose myself seemingly uninvited, but it turned out that *not* joining them was the awkward thing to do.

We got to the town by shared pick-up truck, and when it came time for me to head into the opposite direction I immediately regretted my decision. My new travel buddies asked why I hadn't booked the same place and I didn't have a good answer. We were having fun together so why was I leaving them? I walked off alone with sad violin music playing in my head, feeling like I had rejected them somehow. The next day I moved to the same hostel where we were happily reunited. We continued hanging out together for another week, riding motorbikes around nearby rice fields, visiting waterfalls, hiking through canyons, and having drinks together in the evenings.

Of course, this is not to say that social boundaries don't exist at all, just that they are often more permeable than they are at home. You are obviously still expected to read social cues, and you wouldn't hang out with people if you hadn't established some rapport.

If a group isn't working out or if part of a group would simply like to separate, this usually isn't stated explicitly. Instead, travellers will usually change their travel pace or direction in order to detach from the group. If you find that people are actively changing their plans from yours or your friend's, it is a sign they want to go off and do their own thing. In this case do not cause offence by following them around.

Even if you prefer to do everything on your own, it's still worthwhile to try and chat with people you meet. You can end up having very interesting conversations with people you might normally never have spoken with.

Some examples from my own travels include a former Canadian VIP airline pilot who used to fly around rock stars and CEOs in private jets, and who unsurprisingly had a few good stories to tell. I once met a girl from America who worked in a travelling circus, which was one of the more unusual jobs I have heard of. In Cambodia I met a former Dutch marine who fought the Khmer Rouge back in the 1990s, had seen his buddies die in grenade attacks, and had now come back to Cambodia to see what his sacrifices had meant for the country. In Cuba, I met an Olympic boxing champion while asking for directions. These are not people I would have met at my local grocery store around the corner.

Undoubtedly, if you travel with an open attitude, you will meet many interesting people on your journeys as well.

The Universal Conversation Starter™

But wait, what if you don't know how to meet people? What if you are unsure how to start a conversation? Well, you're in luck, because I have developed a secret 100% guaranteed ice breaker that will universally start a conversation with anyone you meet. This conversation starter is so brilliant that I am in the process of patenting it. I will reveal it to you now:

As soon as you meet another traveller, say the following words: "hey, where are you from?"

That's it! My patent application is not going so well, by the way.

Sure, it may be a bit tired to start with this question, and if you travel a lot you may notice the same conversational patterns repeating themselves. But asking where someone is from is a sure-fire way of starting some chit chat. And if you are meeting a lot of people it can be difficult to remember everyone's name, so it is actually easier to remember them by their country of origin (at least at first).

It may seem a bit out of the blue to ask this question, but many (perhaps even most) interactions between backpackers start out with this phrase. Two other questions that *everyone* asks each other all the time are "where have you been so far?" and, of course, "where are you going?". It's simple, and it works.

If you want to put a different spin on it, make an assumption instead of asking a question. Say, "Hey, you must be from Sweden!" or "You guys must also be heading to Mexico City...". Even if your assumption is wrong you will have just given someone a chance to correct you, which means you have planted the seed for a more proper introduction.

Getting along with other travellers

When travelling the world, you are guaranteed to meet people of all sorts of backgrounds, ages and nationalities, so expect to be reminded of cultural differences on a daily basis. These can be small and innocent ones; a great example is how the phrase "are you alright?" can mean two totally different things coming from a Brit or an American ("hey, how's it going?" versus "are you feeling sick or something?"). Other times you come across fundamental political and cultural differences. Fortunately, in this crazy moveable melting pot, backpackers usually take a relaxed and non-confrontational attitude. Therefore, a great way to get along with people—and this is a cliché, but true—is to just be yourself.

There are however two things that I have noticed in social interactions between backpackers that can get on some people's nerves, and I think they are useful to know about:

Firstly, because everyone introduces themselves by their nationality, there are many opportunities for people to comment on cultural stereotypes. This is not to mean comments that will clearly cause offence (it is common sense to avoid these), but innocent comments that repeatedly come up when a nationality is mentioned. These can get tiring after a while.

For instance, the Swedes don't all want to talk about IKEA, the Dutch don't all want to talk about smoking weed in coffee shops, and the French don't even really want to talk about their cheese and wine. Such topics come up so often that it is helpful to go easy on them, especially when you are just getting to know each other. People often become much more energetic when asking them questions about themselves instead of clichés about their country. (I once met a New Zealander who was so tired of talking about Lord of the Rings that he began telling people he was born on a research station on Antarctica. Though that, of course, eventually got old as well... as there is only so much you can say about penguins or fake scientist parents.)

Another way for conversations to get stifled is when people try to one-up each other in terms of their travel experience. Sometimes a traveller wants to show off or portray themselves as a super hard-core traveller, which can really suck the oxygen out of any conversation. They might reply with a condescending "that's *nice*" to someone who is 'only' in their second week of travelling, or dismiss someone for spending time at a tropical beach while singing their own praises for having gone hiking deep in the mountains. Going off the trail is sometimes seen as having some cachet in backpacker circles, but there really is no right or wrong way to travel. It is best to discourage this kind of pretence by steering the conversation away from it.

While I highlight these two specific issues, the traveller culture is one that is generally very communal, cheerful and inclusive. Mostly you will find that backpackers are wonderful, open and kind people, and that everyone is incredibly invested in sharing stories and having fun.

Hostel dorm etiquette

It's possible you won't be staying in dorms at all, in which case you can happily skip this section. But if you are at all considering sleeping in dorms and want to be a good room-mate, there are a few good practices to observe.

Firstly, say hello to your roomies

People staying in dorms are usually a friendly bunch. While you don't necessarily need to have long conversations with or become everyone's BBF, be sure to give everyone a nice neighbourly greeting. If new people arrive, be sure to say hello to them as well.

Keeps things clean and tidy

Things can get a little disorganized with different bags and piles of clothes around the room, so keep your belongings near your bed. If there's bunk beds and you are sleeping on the lower bed, don't hang up your towel (or all of your laundry) on the ladder as it will annoy your upstairs neighbour who needs to use that ladder.

Avoid making noise at night

Keep things like your toiletries within easy reach and not in, say, a noisy plastic bag, as rummaging through your stuff can wake up others. Partying in a dorm room is usually frowned upon as this is a place for resting or sleeping; instead use the hostel's common room for any late night drinking or socializing.

If you need to leave early in the morning, make sure you pack your bags the day before, and not in the middle of the night. Not only will this be quieter, you easily make mistakes when packing your bags in the dark or when you're only half-awake.

Keep the lights off

People want to sleep, so keep the lights off unless absolutely necessary. Use a flashlight or let a bit of light in from the hallway if you have trouble seeing.

Bring earplugs

Not etiquette but simply a practical matter: make sure you have earplugs on stand-by, in case there's a snorer.

No place for sex

Having sex in a dorm is a bit of a backpacker faux-pas. Fortunately, this very rarely occurs (and when it does it's typically in a crazy 24/7 party hostel), but it's a sure-fire way to make yourself unpopular with the other people. This is especially true if there are bunk beds: you may think you are being quiet, but your down- or upstairs neighbour is going to be very much aware of every movement you make.

Your best bet is to simply get a private room. Of course, sometimes you might just have to make hay while the sun shines, in which case you need to get a bit more creative. Maybe there's a supply closet, rooftop, fire escape or laundry room you can sneak into. A beach can perhaps make for a somewhat more romantic alternative. These places can work in case of carnal emergencies... but in most cases, a private room is the way to go.

Respecting local cultures

As a traveller you are obviously a guest in another country. Respecting local culture is not just the right thing to do but prevents places from becoming spoiled by tourism. As an added bonus, it also leads to locals being generally more helpful and friendly to you. Here are a few ways in which you can respect the local culture.

Learning some local language

You don't have to learn a lot, but try to know at least how to say Hello, Goodbye, Thank You and Excuse Me in the local language. It will show your good intent and will be much appreciated by locals. As far as more advanced language issues go, this will be covered a little bit later in this chapter.

Respecting local customs

Make sure you read up a little on local customs to avoid causing unnecessary offence. Travel guides usually have a section with some pointers on such cultural differences.

I was once in a Buddhist temple where a tour guide had just explained that sitting with your back towards a Buddha statue is considered offensive. Moments later a dozen people were taking group pictures in front of a Buddha statue and, having already forgotten what the guide had said, had their backs and feet towards Buddha. The locals did not complain, perhaps not wanting to make a fuss, but they were visibly annoyed; to them it must have felt like a whole group of people collectively flipping the bird. Situations like this can unfortunately give travellers a bad name.

Local customs can be unusual sometimes. In Thailand, any disrespect towards the King is not only offensive but also against the law. If you find yourself in a movie theatre in Thailand, expect to have to stand up out of respect for the king before the movie begins. A short over-the-top propaganda film will be played showing the king greeting farmers, the king being adored by children, the king gloriously saving kittens from trees, etc., etc. All this may seem strange—he is not *your* king after all—but it's best to just do as everyone does. (It's actually pretty fun.)

Be respectful with your camera as well, as not everyone likes having their picture taken. Either do it on the sly with a telelens, or ask people for permission. People in traditional villages and such sometimes have to endure a lot of photography, and making a bit of a connection with them first is not only respectful but can get you a better portrait of them as well.

Expectations for service

When it comes to restaurant or bar service, we are perhaps a bit spoiled in Western countries. If the service is not sufficiently friendly or efficient, we have every right to complain or withhold a tip.

It doesn't work quite the same everywhere. In many emerging economies the standard of service is lower, to the point of feeling improvised and chaotic by comparison. If you are ordering food with a group of people, don't be surprised when the food doesn't arrive at the same time for everyone.

Waiters may seem rude in some countries, but probably they are just trying to get through your orders quickly. Where they are from, their job may be to simply deliver food to customers, and they might not be expected to also play the role of friendly host. Adjust your expectations for service according to the country you are visiting, and try to approach any problems with a sense of humour.

Dressing appropriately

There is not much of a dress code to worry about in most countries, though there are certain places where you should be mindful about what you are wearing.

When visiting temples or other places of worship you often have to take off your shoes, or you may be denied entry if you wear shorts or a short skirt. In some countries it is considered very rude to walk around shirtless or in a bikini anywhere outside of the immediate vicinity of a beach or pool.

As a woman, it may cause offence to dress in a revealing way in some countries. In this case it is a respectful gesture to cover up the legs or arms, or to wear a sarong or headscarf. In many Muslim countries, this is essentially a must.

Dealing with culture shock

If you are from a high-income country and travelling in low-income regions, you may have to deal with some difficult feelings. Seeing people live in poverty can instil strong feelings of guilt. While they are just scraping by, people in established economies are so much more prosperous that they will even waste money on things they don't really need, or indeed can travel the world just for fun.

If you travel long-term, talking about how long your trip is to someone living in a poor country can truly blow their minds. They may immediately see you as an incredibly rich person, which may be correct from their point of view, but can be very awkward and make it much more difficult to level with them. Sometimes it feels like people have inflated ideas about what Western life is like or how material wealth will lead to happiness. I personally still struggle when responding to questions about the 'dream life' in Europe or America—of course, I don't want to pretend things aren't comfortable there, but I also don't want to suggest we live in a paradise. To be honest, I am still not sure how to approach such issues. Perhaps they are just meant to be awkward.

In some places you may see homeless people or beggars, and even children begging for money or otherwise used as money makers. It is often recommended not to give money to children, as painful as this might be, as it incentives the parents to keep their children begging or working instead of sending them to school.

If you want to help people in a more meaningful or sustainable way, consider giving money to an appropriate charity. Personally, I have been lending money to projects through micro-lending organisations such as Kiva.org, focusing on countries or places that I have felt some personal connection with. Volunteering can be another way to give back.

Spending time with locals

Many travellers wish to meet ordinary locals on their trip who are not employed in the tourist industry, hoping to have more authentic experiences and maybe learn a little bit about another culture.

This is a great goal to have, though don't expect to spontaneously meet locals at every turn. Think of it this way: how often do you speak with or hang out with random travellers in your own home town? This is probably quite rare, or maybe it's never happened before. You have your normal life going on, which is not necessarily going to intersect that often with what visitors might be doing.

Meeting locals requires either a bit of luck, or a bit of determination.

You might just unexpectedly stumble into an amazing local experience. It doesn't happen often, but an opportunity to meet locals could arise at any time, in which case you should definitely jump on it. As a long-term traveller, your chances of hitting the jackpot in this regard are better than for those on a shorter holiday focused only on the most touristy places.

Meeting locals can be one of the most fun parts of travelling, and can leave you grinning from ear to ear when recalling such experiences later.

One time in Argentina, I met some locals while watching a football match in a sports bar. The next day I found myself joining them at a BBQ in someone's garden, which turned into an epic eating marathon lasting an incredible twelve hours. It was a true education on the Argentinians' unending love for grilled meat, and a wonderful day shared with some of the most welcoming people I've ever met. I still send them my greetings from time to time.

Once, in a remote little village in The Philippines, I was unexpectedly invited to eat with a local family. We joined in the family prayer and ate rice with pig skin, which they had insisted on sharing (it was delicious—and to return the favour we bought everyone some quality beers they couldn't ordinarily afford). We then spent the evening under a bamboo roof telling each other stories, drinking coconut wine, and singing songs. The kids showed me crabs and frogs they had caught in the river and invited me to come along fishing the next morning. We were later joined by the village fool, a skinny old man who somewhat resembled Michael Jackson in the *Thriller* music video, and who kept boasting about being a ladies' man. It doesn't get much better than this.

When you do end up spending time with locals beyond the usual pleasantries, cherish these occasions. It is rare to be given a window into how people live in another country, instead of only seeing the tourist-facing side. Take an interest in everyone, play the role of cultural ambassador, and of course be gracious to your hosts.

Simply stumbling upon such an experience is rare, however. Fortunately, there are also some other ways in which you won't leave it to chance, and can meet locals in a more deliberate way. Here are some of them:

Meeting local guides

Many sites have sprung up over the past few years aiming to connect travellers with local amateur guides. The idea is that, for a fee, a local will show you around their home town. The concept is very similar to room-sharing sites like Airbnb, but for experiences instead of accommodation.

The three major players at the time of writing are Vayable (www.vayable.com), GetYourGuide (www.getyourguide.com) and WithLocals (www.withlocals.com).

Meeting up with friends-of-friends

Why not use your own social network to see if anyone might know a local in a place you are going? See if you can connect with a friend-of-a-friend, maybe offering to take them out for food or drinks so you can ask them for recommendations on cool places to check out.

A Thai picnic in Bangkok (WithLocals.com)

Hospitality exchanges (e.g. Couchsurfing)

In hospitality exchanges, locals share a room or couch with travellers completely for free, with the expectation of cultural exchange, or to build up a profile within the community so they can stay for free when they are travelling in the future. Couchsurfing (www.couchsurfing.com) is, by far, the biggest hospitality exchange. There are always questions regarding safety, which Couchsurfing addresses well on its own site. Many local Couchsurfing communities also organise free weekly or monthly meet-ups in places all around the world, which are great events for meeting people.

TrustRoots (www.trustroots.org) is another hospitality exchange community for hitch-hikers and other travellers. Trampolinn (www.trampolinn.com) is another take on the concept, except here you can earn and 'spend" virtual points based on how often you have hosted people and how often you have been a guest.

Homestays

Homestays are a type of paid accommodation connecting guests with live-in hosts who open their homes to travellers. It's the perfect way to stay with a local family and learn a bit about their way of life and taste the local and regional dishes. Sometimes you sleep in a separate annex, or sometimes you sleep in a room in the same house as the family.

The goal of a homestay is specifically to achieve cultural immersion, and sometimes homestays are offered in combination with language classes. The term homestay is typically used in more rural places than urban ones: think farmhouses, not condos.

There is sometimes a little confusion over what a homestay means. In Indonesia, some hostels call themselves homestays only for tax reasons, without actually offering a family experience. In Vietnam I once stayed in a "home stay" that was really just a budget hotel... "Welcome to my home!", the owner said, as he gestured towards a dozen purpose-built bungalows. Check what is actually being offered to avoid disappointment.

Location-based online dating (e.g. Tinder)

Don't laugh! Dating apps such as Tinder can be powerful tools to meet locals. This can be with romantic intention or without (so long as you manage expectations, of course). Not just for hook-ups, these apps can get you in touch with many locals quickly. In your profile, make it clear that you are a visitor in town until so-and-so, and be specific about wanting to meet locals or being interested in language exchange. You could specify that you're not actually looking for dates, or of course you could leave this open.

Language exchanges

Learning a language can be a perfect excuse for meeting locals as well. Sometimes such exchanges are even organised by backpacker hostels, though this depends on which country you are in and the overall demand. There are many language exchanges organised in Latin America for example—as there are plenty of locals wanting to improve their English as well as plenty of travellers wanted to improve their Spanish.

Volunteering on a farm

WWOOF (www.wwoof.net) is an organisation that places volunteers on organic farms in over 50 countries around the world. 'WWOOFing' has become a popular way to live like a local for a while. You will be expected to do daily chores on a farm for a week up to several months, while receiving meals and a place to sleep for free. In addition to learning about organic farming, you can learn about the local ecology and culture while getting to meet fun and interesting people.

Other ways to meet locals

Clearly this list is not exhaustive and you might find other ways to have local experiences. For instance, sometimes you might meet domestic tourists who are going on the same tours or activities as you are.

The second best thing to meeting locals is meeting expats who live somewhere temporarily. These might even be people from your home country who have gained much local knowledge abroad. Joining an expat community, even briefly, can let you see a different side of a city or region than you would normally see.

Dealing with language barriers

The thought of going to a foreign country where the language is not their own can send some people spiralling into severe anxiety. For others it is no big deal, even if they're far from language geniuses.

Where you come from can hugely affect your attitude towards communicating in foreign places. The Dutch, Germans or Scandinavians for instance, who have lots of mandatory language classes in school and deal often with people from their neighbouring countries, seem not to care much about language barriers at all. They shrug and get on with it, improvising if necessary. Travellers from many English-speaking countries seem to more commonly experience discomfort with language barriers, to a point where they might avoid certain parts of the world for this reason alone (which is a huge shame).

The key to dealing with language barriers is not, as you might think, knowing more languages or being better at languages. That clearly helps, but that's not the *real* issue. The key is not to be embarrassed to try. If you can get over yourself and are okay with making yourself a little vulnerable, you will be amazed by how much you can communicate regardless of the situation.

Communicating in English

If English is your first language, or if you can speak it as your second language, then congratulations! You know one of the most useful languages around. You will be able to speak with the vast majority of people in the UK, US, Canada, Australia, South Africa and 19 other countries in Africa, places all over the Caribbean, India, and a handful of other Asian countries. Not bad for a freebie.

Some level of English is also taught and spoken all over the world as it is obviously the international *lingua franca*. Take Europe, for instance. The percentage of people speaking English as a second language in continental Europe is over 90% in The Netherlands and the Nordic countries, over 50% in Germany, Belgium, Austria, Greece and Switzerland, and somewhere around 30% elsewhere in Europe. Again, not bad! You will be easily able to survive here.

Of course, English is not widely spoken as a second language everywhere. Even when people do know some English, they might not always be very good at it. It is up to you to assess the skill level of the person you are speaking with, and adapt your English to their level.

This seems like an obvious point, but it is often poorly understood. Instead of simplifying their English so the other person can understand them more easily, some travellers will raise their volume or even start shouting. The problem is clearly not that someone is hard of hearing, but that the level of English is too complicated or too fast for them to follow.

Such issues show that while knowing English can be useful, you often won't get far without knowing another 'language' as well: that of Pidgin (simplified) English...

A crash course in Pidgin English

When dealing with people with limited English skills, always keep things simple.

Let's say you are in an artisinal cheese shop in a country where English is not commonly spoken. Don't tell the person behind the counter, "Good day sir, I thought I would infiltrate your place of purveyance to negotiate the vending of some cheesy comestibles!"

Okay, that much is probably clear. But even saying, "Hello, me and my friend and I are wondering if you have any cheese for sale" might be equally impenetrable to a basic English speaker. It can sound as verbose and overly complicated to them as the earlier sentence is to you.

Still getting blank stares? Simplify further: "Hello. We want to buy cheese." Maybe that sounds a little forward, a little rude even, but it does get straight to the point. Say basic things like want or need, instead of "wish", "would like to", or "wondering".

Don't be afraid to regress all the way down to caveman language if needed (but only if it's clear the other person's English knowledge is at the extreme beginner level). Forget about past or future tense or conjugating verbs. Focus on combining a common verb with a common noun. "We buy cheese?". "Looking for food!" "Need hotel." "Going to mountain." Say it with a smile and it will come across as friendly, even if it sounds very blunt.

Bear in mind that you are not offending people by speaking in a very basic way—unless they are clearly proficient in English, of course. You are merely doing them a service by making yourself more easily understandable to them. As a guest in their country, this is your responsibility.

Another key element of Pidgin English is the ability to slow down your speech. Maybe the person you are dealing with actually knows a surprising amount of English, but they just need you speak a little bit slower so they can actually parse what you are saying. Never RAISE YOUR VOICE AS THIS IS SUPER RUDE, instead... just try speaking... a little bit slower. You can also try *emphasizing*... a key word.

Picture, for a moment, the way a stoner talks. "You know, dude... how... like... everything... is connected, man?" Emulate this rhythm of speech and you will make yourself vastly more understandable. Be sure to also put pauses between sentences to give the other person some time to process. Maybe speed things up *slightly* from pure stoner level, and you should be golden. If it seems like people are easily following everything you are saying, you can dial up the speed a bit.

Simply speaking more slowly can open many doors for you. People with basic English knowledge will love you for it. They will compliment you on how patient and wonderful a person you are. Make any attempt at learning a few words in their language while you are at it, and you will instantly become their favourite person. (As a side note, if you are single and want to get in with all those sexy foreigners, being patient and speaking a bit more slowly can make you a superstar. Do not underestimate these powers.)

Hmmm, maybe that language barrier isn't so terrible after all...

Non-verbal communication

But what if you're in a situation where English gets you zero mileage at all, even when used in its most basic forms? Fret not, as you can still rely on non-verbal communication.

What this requires is, again, a willingness to embarrass yourself just a bit. Put yourself in a vulnerable position by attempting to communicate using gestures or sounds. If that makes you self-conscious at all, know that most people will not find this weird, and at worst will simply find it endearing.

If you are in that hypothetical cheese shop from the previous section, you can obviously express your desire to buy some cheese by pointing at it and looking at the vendor expectantly.

Need to communicate a number? Just hold up a certain number of fingers, or pretend to write the number with your index finger on the palm of your hand.

Hungry? Make a gesture as though you are spooning food into your mouth, or pat your stomach.

Need a place to sleep? Rest your head sideways on your hand as though you are resting your head on a pillow, and look in a few different directions with a quizzical look. Even a child will understand this.

Want to express your thanks? Place your hand in your heart or make a respectful little nod.

What's the time? Tap your wrist.

Money? Rub your thumb and fingers together.

Is the food not what you ordered? Point at your food and furrow your brow, then point at the menu. The waiter will no doubt rush to correct their mistake.

Of course, these are just some examples. If you approach things with imagination and humour, you will be amazed at how much you can communicate even with limited or no use of language.

Ordering food can be difficult when using English is not an option, but sign language is always there in a pinch. In Vietnam I once ordered chicken soup by clucking like a chicken and pointing at another customer's bowl of soup. In Guatemala, before I knew the words "huevos fritos", I ordered my eggs fried by pointing at eggs on the menu and drawing a circle inside another circle on the tablecloth with my finger (i.e. the yolk and egg-white). The waitress got it immediately.

Sometimes a little initiative is needed. After repeated failed attempts at ordering food at a small roadside restaurant in Myanmar, I simply walked into the kitchen (to the delight of the cooks) and pointed at anything that smelled good. Another solution is to get another customer who knows some English to order for you—not only will that take care of the ordering, but they will probably know what's good on the menu!

Point-It Dictionaries

Still concerned about language issues? Then there's one more option: bring a Point-It dictionary. This is a little booklet containing illustrations of hundreds of objects and concepts. To communicate a basic idea to someone, all you have to do is open your dictionary and point at a picture. Besides the pocket-size paper versions, you can also get point-it dictionaries as apps for your smartphone.

Learning other languages

Finally, a sure-fire way to communicate with locals is to try and learn their language instead of relying on them to use yours.

How much time and energy you wish to invest in learning a local language probably depends on how long you are staying and how useful that skill will be elsewhere. Learning Thai makes sense if you're going to live in Thailand for a while, but for a 3 week stay it won't exactly pay off—nor will you be able to use much Thai elsewhere around the world later. Learning a couple of Thai phrases (hello, goodbye, thank you, etc.) will be useful in showing your respect to the locals, but learning more might be too much of an investment.

On the other hand, learning Spanish if you're in Latin America for a while can pay huge dividends, as few people in this part of the world know English. You will be able to better communicate with the locals, and you can keep using your Spanish knowledge throughout 21 different Spanish-speaking countries. Many backpackers following the Gringo Trail start knowing not a single word, but find themselves able to hold a conversation in Spanish pretty well by the end of their journey.

Similarly, knowing at least a few awkward bits of Mandarin can make a world of difference when travelling in China, and given China's growing importance in the world it is surely not useless knowledge to have. Then again, language learning does not always have to serve a greater purpose, and maybe you want to do it just for the fun of it.

Once again, the key to communicating in a new language is to not be embarrassed. You are clearly going to be terrible at a language at first, and that's okay. Don't hold out until you think you can deliver beautiful and grammatically perfect sentences, as that could be forever; start using a language in whatever way you can straight away. If you expect people to laugh at you for sounding stupid, know that the reaction you get 99% of the time is simply a smile and an appreciation that, hey, at least you are trying. There's no point in going for perfect volleys at first—all you are trying to do is just to get the ball over the net, no matter how awkwardly!

Here are some ways in which you can learn languages as you travel:

- **Most guidebooks contain phrase lists**, which are a decent place to start.
- **Bringing a dedicated phrasebook** can help as well. This won't really help you learn the language, but it can help you memorize some prefab phrases.

- **You can get language classes locally.** (For as little as $100 a week, you can get private Spanish tutoring in many Latin American countries.)
- **Put a dictionary app on your phone**, and look up any words or phrases that you encounter on your travels.
- **Listen to audio courses.** You will be spending a lot of time in transit anyway, so this can be a great time to use for language learning.
- **Go to language exchanges.** Great for meeting locals as well.
- **Use free interactive learning sites** and apps like Duolingo (www.duolingo.com) or Memrise (www.memrise.com)

A huge resource for language learning is the website Fluent In 3 Months (www.fluentin3months.com). It is run by a guy who travels to a new country every three months, where he attempts to become conversationally fluent in the local language. The blog is incredibly inspirational and full of advice and resources.

Key points from this chapter

- Who you travel with, or whether you travel alone, has a huge impact on your travel experience. **Make sure you are compatible with your travel companions.**
- Social interactions work a bit differently in backpacker culture than it might at home. Don't be surprised when people are very easy-going when making introductions or doing things together.
- **Avoid harping on cultural stereotypes** or competing for who is the most 'seasoned traveller' and your interactions with other backpackers will go much smoother.
- Be mindful of others when staying in dorms.
- **Be respectful to local customs and laws.** Dress appropriately, learn some local language, and approach any issues with patience and humour. You will find that most people are extremely nice to travellers, especially when you show an open and inquisitive attitude.
- There are many different ways to **meet locals** in the countries you're visiting. Meeting locals can be a great way to learn more about other cultures and get out of the 'traveller bubble'.

- You can often **creatively deal with language barriers**, for instance by pointing, using gestures, or by using a point-it dictionary.
- When speaking English to people with limited English abilities, **be sure to speak slowly and to simplify your language**. Never start shouting or raising your voice. Speaking clearly and slowly will be hugely appreciated by locals who speak English as a second language.

11

How to travel solo

MANY PEOPLE SADLY still think of travel as something you only do with friends or with a partner. Solo travel, surely, is only for the hardcore vagabonds who play the harmonica and have birds living in their hair.

Before I set out on my first long-term solo trip, I admittedly felt a bit self-conscious about it. I expected I would have to explain my circumstances to people... explain why I could not share this trip with a friend or partner, and why I am doing this 'all on my own'.

A few days into that trip, I realized I wasn't the unique and courageous little snowflake I thought I was. I met other solo travellers virtually everywhere I went; in some places it even seemed like solo was the default mode of travel, and those travelling together were in the minority. Rather than having to explain myself or having in any way 'deal with' travelling solo, I quickly got to see it as something very natural, very accepted and also very exciting. There is, honestly, nothing weird about travelling solo.

But it *is* a little bit scary.

A solo traveller has to be very self-reliant. There is only one person responsible for every decision, and that person is you. Fear of loneliness can also be difficult to deal with, and many first-time solo traveller worry if they are only going to have themselves for company the whole time.

Recognizing that solo travel can be a bit more difficult than travelling together (at least initially), this chapter will go through some steps you can take to make solo travel work for you. Ultimately, it is somewhat of an acquired skill and it is not for everyone, but it also not as challenging as many people think.

One of the great advantages of solo travel is that you are no longer dependent on others to travel. Sometimes your friends just aren't able to join you due to work or other obligations, and it is especially rare for friends to both be in a situation allowing them to get away for a longer-term trip. Solo travel, by the way, is not only for those who are single. Some people travel both with their partner and on their own.

Personally, I think it may just be the best way to travel, and hope to convince more people to do it.

Why solo is my favourite way to travel

Solo may be the best way to travel when you're going on a big journey. At the very least, it is a unique way of travelling that will give you a very different perspective, and one that everyone should probably try at least once.

What's great about travelling solo is that you can be completely free of obligations and compromises. You don't have to be anything to anybody, so if you want to take a break from travelling and just party for a week, there is no one stopping you. Or if you want to climb the tallest mountain, go ahead and show that mountain who's boss.

Having no one to answer to but yourself also opens you up to new experiences. I think over time our personalities develop many defaults that we fall back on, which get reinforced continuously because the people we know already expect us to behave in certain ways. When I'm travelling solo, it feels like I am writing on a blank slate. It is easier to push against my comfort zone and to try new things.

It is sometimes suggested that solo travel is a selfish endeavour, and to be honest, on some level it probably is a little bit. But solo travel also invites you to connect more with your surroundings, to be more in the moment, and to connect more with other people. I often find myself having conversations I wouldn't have had otherwise, or having moments of quiet introspection during which I notice things that would have normally passed me by.

Solo is not the same as alone

There is a common misconception that solo travel must be a lonely ordeal. Some people have told me I am "brave" for going solo. While I do think it is brave to *decide* to travel solo, I do not think the actual act of solo travel requires that much courage.

To be fair, it can be the kind of isolated ordeal that some people imagine it to be, but this depends largely on where you are going. A friend of mine went backpacking through Siberia, and her stories made it sound like a very tough place to be on your own. The locals there didn't appreciate foreigners at all, so much so that ticket-windows at train stations would close for people who didn't look Russian. My friend didn't meet other travellers for days, even weeks, in the ice cold wastelands. Such solitude can have its own kind of appeal, but it's a calibre of travel that is not for everyone.

The reality in more popular backpacking destinations, of which I have mentioned many throughout this book, is very different. There you will find that travel is very social, if that is what you want it to be. Locals in popular backpacking countries are much more used to seeing foreigners, so interacting with them is easier. And if you use the Universal Conversation Starter™ from the previous chapter, you will quickly find yourself spending time with many other backpackers. You might in fact meet so many people, that from time to time you'll want to be alone by choice just to have a little recharge.

Practically speaking, solo travel is now easier than it has ever been. If you were travelling solo to far-away lands in, say, the 70ies, you would be truly going off the grid. Your family might hear from you only through the occasional postcard, or maybe a brief chat through a costly international phone connection. Any problems you encountered on the road would have to be solved there and then. These days, the internet is available pretty much everywhere, so if you are ever stuck there are always resources to consult or people to reach.

If you are thinking of travelling solo for the first time, be sure to you choose your destination well. Clearly, avoid places like Siberia if you don't want to be alone often. Instead, pick a popular backpacking destination and you are bound to find yourself in good company a lot of the time.

How to enjoy being on your own

Wait, didn't we just establish that solo travel can be a very fun and social activity, and that you probably are going to meet lots of people given that you pick the right destination? Yes, but...

In order to make friends on the road and feel truly comfortable in your own skin, I believe you first need to be okay with being alone. It may sound counter-intuitive, but I think the people who are the least capable of enjoying their own company struggle the most to make connections. As the great Master Yoda once said, "Meet people you want, be comfortable alone you must." (Sorry, I just love Yoda grammar.)

Not meeting people can be a bit like a self-fulfilling prophecy. Sometimes there is someone in the hostel who seems clearly uncomfortable on their own, and I have to admit that I am instinctively not drawn to talking to that person... at least not straight away. They are in a negative frame of mind, which is easy to pick up even subconsciously. Now, I know that this person is actually who I should want to speak to the most (and usually I do), but I recognize that my stupid reptilian brain tells me otherwise.

I think it's just the way human beings are wired up. We subtly pick up vibes from others, and if they don't immediately resonate with us, we hesitate to make contact. The opposite is also true; if I see someone who seems really content and relaxed on their own, I am much more inclined to have a chat. This is part of why it is important to be okay being on your own.

There also is just inherent value in being able to enjoy your own company. It can be really great to have some quality me-time. For instance, one of my favourite activities is to explore a city on my own, because there is really no better way to constantly indulge your curiosity.

Sometimes there is simply no one else around, in which case you should be able to have fun regardless. Needing to be around people to have fun only makes yourself dependent on an outside factor you cannot always control.

Here are a few specific things you can do to make your alone-time more enjoyable:

- **Be in the moment.** Rather than thinking about the future or the past, try to be in the present. Give yourself some time to enjoy that beautiful view of the mountains, or grab a drink in a local coffee house and spend some time people-watching. Try to put yourself in a mindful state and suck up the colours of the world through your eyes.

- **Take photos.** I find that photography is a wonderful way to engage with my surroundings. When I am photographing, I notice many things that otherwise I would not have, and often these are things that make me smile.

- **Interact with locals.** Try to chat with staff, salespeople and waiters. Greet people on the street if they seem friendly. If you are in a less-travelled area where people don't often see strangers, you will often be met with a lot of friendly curiosity. Walk through a village in, say, rural Indonesia, and chances are every kid in town will want to high-five you as you pass. Enjoy these encounters.

- **Bring a book.** When I am travelling with other people I rarely find any time to read. When I am on my own, I welcome the chance to dig into a good book. I will take it with me even when I am sightseeing, so that I can break up my day with some reading if I feel like.

- **Share your stories online.** Write something about your adventures and share it with your friends or family back home. This is a great way to process your day even if you don't have anyone to talk with.

- **Listen to music.** Add a soundtrack to whatever you are doing and it will instantly feel like you are in your own movie. Even walking around town can become a cinematic experience if you listen to some good tunes. You can even literally listen to a movie soundtrack while exploring a place; one of the best things I ever did was to walk around Shibuya district in Tokyo while listening to the soundtrack of Lost in Translation.

- **Eat in restaurants.** Being alone should not stop you from sitting down and enjoying some nice food. Don't feel like you have to go to a fast-food place where you will be in and out quickly; find a restaurant with a casual atmosphere and plop yourself down. Having a proper meal is a nice time to reflect, and you often can use Wi-Fi or read a book while you are waiting.

How to make friends

If you are reasonably sociable and if you choose your destination well, you will find that meeting people becomes almost inevitable. However, there are some ways to make encounters with other backpackers more likely:

- **Stay in hostel dorms.** Sharing a room with others in a hostel is the surest way of making friends, so don't be a hermit by staying in hotels all the time. The highest-rated hostels on sites like Hostel-World.com are ones where you are bound to meet lots of people.

- **Pick a hostel that has a bar or common room.** Hostel bars often have a wonderfully inclusive atmosphere, with many people socializing or playing games. Introduce yourself to someone and before you know it you will be chatting with a whole group of people.

- **Talk to people when in transit.** Bus and train journeys can be long and people will typically be a bit bored, so this is a perfect time for a friendly chat. I often make new friends while I am in transit, and sometimes the people I meet on the bus, boat or train will be people I end up staying in the same hostel with.

- **Go on group activities.** Book a guided tour, or a cooking class, or some other group activity. Often this is a perfect way to socialize. Try booking activities through a hostel before trying with a more general travel agency to increase the chances of meeting similar types of travellers.

- **Use social networks.** Some backpackers use sites like travbuddy.com to find travel buddies in advance of their trip. It might work well for you, though I am personally skeptical of these platforms for one simple reason: you won't know if you will actually get along with someone, but by formalizing your connection through a site, you will probably feel obligated to stick together even when it's not working out so well. It's easier to team up with, and part ways with, people you meet serendipitously. That said, when you are in a hub location such as a capital you could organize a traveller meet-up by posting a message through an online community. CouchSurfing also organizes regular group meet-ups in many large cities.

Speaking of social networks, it is a good idea to add people on Facebook who you particularly connect with on your trip. Even if you are taking different routes, there may be opportunities to meet up again in the future.

Making connections can sometimes be tough, but one connection can quickly lead to another. For instance, once you have spoken to one person in a hostel bar or common room you will probably be introduced to others, or you can both introduce yourselves to others together. Remember this potential snowball effect when arriving somewhere new, and don't be too hard on yourself if you are not making connections as easily as you did before.

The downsides of solo travel

While solo is my favourite way to travel, it is not without its drawbacks.

The first one is purely financial: you will be paying twice as much for a private room than a couple who are sharing. Transportation and activities are also more expensive when the cost is not divided among multiple people. This can fortunately be somewhat offset by sleeping in dorm beds at least part of the time, and by sharing accommodation, transportation and activities with other travellers (solo or otherwise) whenever you can.

The other downside is that while you will have many more peak experiences, the emotional valleys can also be deeper, and inevitably you will have a few bad days.

Maybe you just find yourself in an uninspiring place. Even if you are okay being on your own, and even if you typically do manage to meet other people, you may still feel a bit off or lonely sometimes. It's important to accept these days for what they are and to quickly shrug them off. As the saying goes: shit happens. Have faith that the situation can change entirely tomorrow.

When I first got to The Philippines I didn't manage to socialize with anyone. I had parted ways with some long-time travel buddies in Singapore, and despite trying to make some new friends my heart just wasn't in it. Manila had me down as it's not the nicest of places. To make matters worse I got food poisoning and vomited all over the hostel's brand new carpet—and so I became 'that guy'. Fortunately, I knew this was one of those emotional valleys, and instead of dwelling on it I decided to spend some time reading a book. A few days later, I had some of my most memorable and rewarding travel adventures when visiting the stunning islands around Palawan together with two other backpackers. This is a perfect example of how your situation can shift dramatically from day to day.

A bad day can easily be turned around by giving yourself a break. Don't dwell on it and don't compare your current situation to how great everything used to be somewhere else: just accept it as inevitable and make a plan to shake things up tomorrow. Relax, go for a swim or read a book, and focus on what still lies ahead.

Getting through the first few days

I subscribe to a few travel forums, such as /r/solotravel on Reddit.com, and every now and then I see a panicked post from someone who is travelling solo for the first time and feeling way in over their head. This usually happens on their first or second day, and is typically triggered by something minor not quite going their way. Maybe it was difficult to find their hotel, maybe they missed a bus connection, or maybe they just suddenly feel very alone.

It's understandable. Going on a big journey on your own can feel a bit like jumping into the deep without yet knowing how to swim. As you step off that plane you may be thinking, "Holy crap, what am I doing?". Getting through the first few days can be a little tough.

My first time travelling solo was when went to California for a week when I was 17. I had never been to another continent before and it was only my second time flying. When I arrived at LAX airport I immediately felt lost. I never had to deal with jetlag before, so I was unfamiliar with that foggy state of mind. On top of that, being in a big city I only knew from the movies felt surreal and detached. What actually set off my minor freak-out was some whooshing in my ear—I didn't yet know this happens sometimes when you fly with a cold, and I actually thought I was losing my hearing.

I was about to call my parents who were probably sleeping at the time, but fortunately stopped myself and took a deep breath. I calmed myself down, and simply focused on meeting up with several people I was supposed to meet. Over the next two days I still had to deal with some insomnia and lack of appetite, but my jetlag subsided, my ears stopped whooshing, and I ended up having an amazing time. The people I met turned out to be awesome and some are still friends of mine today. I went on to travel internationally almost every year since.

When you arrive in a new place, the most important thing to do is to give yourself some time to acclimatize, so don't put too much pressure on those first few days. Of course you are going to be a bit lost and disoriented. After all, you are outside of your comfort zone, so let yourself be scared for a bit. Take a deep breath and slowly push through. Get used to your new surroundings, gradually start exploring, and remember to be proud that you are doing something new and exciting.

Most problems can be dealt with by approaching them pragmatically. If you don't like a place, go somewhere else. If there is no one in your hostel to talk to, go to a different hostel. You are in control, so it is all up to you.

Even though I have now travelled solo many times, I still get a tiny bit nervous before departing on a solo trip. It's now more of a case of butterflies in my stomach than any actual anxiety, but I still can't help but wonder if maybe this solo trip will be different from the other ones. Invariably, I quickly get back into the spirit of things and end up having a blast.

What if you are very shy?

If you are not a naturally sociable person, you may think all this talk about solo travel does not apply to you. Actually, I think in some ways solo travel is more relevant to you than if you aren't a little shy.

I am very sociable nowadays but I grew up an introvert. I liked playing with Lego or playing video games on my own, but many social situations would make me really awkward. For a time, I didn't much like birthday parties, even my own, because I never knew how to act in such a group setting. However, over the years my personality changed a lot, and I think challenging myself to do scary things sometimes (like deciding to travel solo) contributed a lot to this change.

These days I have no issues talking to strangers, I am a comfortable public speaker and can even be a social butterfly when I am in the mood. I am still a bit awkward every now and then, as my friends can probably attest, but maybe some things never change.

Travel can be a great way to break out of your shell. Solo travel will certainly be more difficult if you are shy, but also all the more rewarding once you get the hang of it.

The key is not to expect everything to work out straight away. Learning to travel solo is a bit like going on your first workout at the gym... the first time will be difficult, you will easily be out of breath and your muscles will be painful afterwards. But... no pain, no gain. A few more visits to the gym and your workout goes a lot smoother. A few more visits still and suddenly those weights don't feel as heavy anymore, and exercising starts to make you feel really great. Solo travel, like training a muscle, is something you need to build up a bit.

If solo travel feels daunting, try taking little steps first. Explore a city in your country on your own for a day and see how it feels. Or sign up to a course in your area and get used to the idea of showing up by yourself. Maybe hold off on doing that huge solo trip and test the waters a bit first, as you will be better prepared.

There are various group tour operators that are popular with solo travellers. Companies like Contiki and Top Deck focus on younger age groups, and there are other companies targeting older demographics. Organized group tours are a great way of doing something on your own while also knowing you will be quickly introduced to many people. It's a bit like solo travel with training wheels, as you don't have to worry about your itinerary or your day-to-day decision-making and can focus all your attention on making connections and having fun.

If you still struggle travelling solo, make sure you give it your best shot. If it *really* doesn't work out, then at least you will have learned something about yourself. You can always decide to go back and travel with a friend or partner next time.

Key points from this chapter

- There is absolutely **nothing weird about traveling solo**, and lots of people do it.
- **Traveling solo isn't the same as traveling alone**, nor does it have to mean you are a loner. It can be an incredibly fun and social way to travel. Many solo travellers form ad hoc groups on the trail.
- **Solo travel has many advantages**. You can make your journey completely your own, and you will be more open to experiences that will pass by those who are on a journey together.
- However, you will also need to get accustomed to making friends on the road as well as spending time alone sometimes.
- **Where you are going matters a lot**. Staying in hostels in Asia or South America will be easy, travelling in Siberia or sleeping in motels on a US road trip will be hard, so pick your destinations wisely (or at least know what to expect).

12

Coming back home

EVENTUALLY YOU WILL HAVE to face the inevitable. Eventually, you will have to go home.

As your return flight takes off and you look out the airplane window, you will no doubt be reflecting on your journey. Perhaps you wished you could have travelled longer, or perhaps you felt that by now it was time to go home.

Regardless of whether you were ready to go back, your homecoming will no doubt have its challenges...

Keeping memories alive

Something that will really aid the transition back into normal life is to try and hold onto all of those wonderful travel memories you surely have collected. Keep some records or mementos of your trip, such as photos, videos, or journal entries.

Be sure to take a camera with you on your journey. If you don't have much experience with photography, consider taking a course or reading a how-to book before your trip. After all, it's a shame when your photos have to be accompanied with disclaimers like "it was much more impressive in person" or "trust me, it was really beautiful". Fortunately, a little learning goes a long way in improving the quality of your pictures.

For longer trips, I also recommend keeping a personal diary or logbook for later reading. Mind you, it's not necessary to write incredible prose, nor do you have to glamorize your experiences in your writing. In fact, doing so risks sucking the life out of those experiences, and it can even cause you to procrastinate because of the writing effort seemingly involved. Instead, try to keep some quick scribbles about particularly interesting moments, people you met, food you ate, or other things you want to remember. With so many experiences compressed into a single journey everything can quickly start to blur together, but even some brief notes can bring back focus to all those different individual memories.

Reverse culture shock

Coming back from a long journey can be difficult. When I came back from my first long-term trip, I was surprised to actually feel nothing at first. I wasn't that relieved to be back, nor depressed that it was all over... I just felt nothing. Whereas all of my senses were constantly engaged during my journey, I felt numb upon return. London, where I lived at the time, is far from a dull city, but I found myself just moving through it on auto-pilot. Perhaps my brain had been so overstimulated for so long that it was now incapable of processing sensory input at more regular levels.

That said, it's a joy to reunite with friends and family you have missed. And after staying in hostels and hotel rooms for so long, collapsing into a couch and just watching some TV can be glorious. Once you are somewhat settled in again, that first week can feel extremely familiar and cosy, like tucking yourself in under a comfy duvet (literally or figuratively).

This feeling can be short-lived however, and by week two you may already be longing back to your travelling days.

One of the surreal things about coming back is that seemingly time stood still while you were away. A lot of people will tell you it's "same old, same old". They still complain about that same job, are still annoyed with their morning commute, and are still thinking of maybe renovating the kitchen sometime. For you, having had the experience of a lifetime, things are far from same old.

Upon return you will undoubtedly be excited to share all your travel stories, but having gained so many you will surely bounce all over the place: from that one time you did that thing in Mumbai to that other time in that desert in Mexico oh and of course when you were scuba diving in Colombia. Much to your friends' frustration, you will struggle to resist one-upping their anecdotes with something way more amazing that happened on your travels. Sure, their commute to work might have been a nightmare this morning, but what was *really* a nightmare was taking that night bus in Laos... *funny story, actually...*

While your friends will want to hear some of your stories, no one wants every conversation to be dominated by high tales of your adventures. If your journey left a strong impression on you, for a while you might just be that person who tells people "I have changed, man... I have changed" while looking wistfully into the distance. It is okay to slap yourself when this happens (I certainly had to a few times). It's difficult for people to relate fully to your changed perspectives if they have not had similar experiences as well.

If you have been travelling to lower-cost regions of the world, re-adjusting to prices in Western countries can be a challenge. When I went to the supermarket again for the first time I had to stop myself before putting a roll of bin bags in my shopping basket, because I realized this roll of flimsy recycled plastic cost as much as three dinner meals in Indonesia. I was ready to shake my fist and yell, "This is an outrage!", but begrudgingly paid the astronomical price of three British pounds.

Similarly, the price of a beer in a pub will suddenly seem utterly absurd: at least £4 versus about 50p to £1 in many backpacking countries. For a while I was reluctant to pay for things even if I could afford them, and it took a month or two for me to stop obsessing over prices.

What's next?

It's good to have a plan for when you come back. Ideally, start working on a plan in advance of your return. Take a look at your CV again, or start reacquainting yourself with your course materials, or whatever else your daily life will soon involve. If you quit your job or gave up your apartment to travel, start looking at job openings or a place to rent some time in advance.

To get through the initial post-trip phase, it can be both fun and therapeutic to reminisce with your travel partner(s) from time to time. Try staying in touch with some of the people you met on your journey, as well. Even if they live far away, social media makes it easy to stay in touch.

It's even better to keep the backpacking spirit alive, if only in small ways. Strolling through a funky neighbourhood and discovering some new art galleries or shops can remind you of your days as an explorer. There may well be sights or activities near you that you had not thought of going before. When I last came back to England, I opened the WikiVoyage page for my city just for fun, and realized I had never been to the stunning Seven Sisters cliffs along the channel sea, even though they were just a stone's throw away from where I lived. It's funny how we often ignore the things that are right in front of us. Undoubtedly there are some great things to see in your home country that you might have overlooked.

Finally, of course, you can start planning your next trip. Dreaming about all the places you have yet to see can make for some great post-travel therapy. Now that you have had the experience of a lifetime, your next trip might even be inevitable. As Michael Palin once put it: "Once the travel bug bites there is no known antidote, and I know that I shall be happily infected until the end of my life."

I hope you will be happily infected too.

Afterword

I hope you enjoyed this book and that it has helped you prepare for your travels. If so, please recommend it to others, as this book is self-published and relies entirely on word-of-mouth.

Better yet, post a review online so that more people can discover this book! I would be very grateful for your honest review. Amazon is the largest platform for book and e-book sales and so a review on Amazon is enormously valuable. The best places to leave a review are Amazon US and Amazon UK, and you can leave a review here even if you purchased the book elsewhere. (The digital version of this book is also available through Kobo, Nook, Apple iBook Store, Scribd, Page Foundry and IndieTraveller.co.)

If you would like to get in touch, my e-mail address is marek@indietraveller.co. I also invite you to visit www.indietraveller.co, where I blog about my travels and where you can find a lot of additional travel information.

You can leave a review on the Amazon US page: http://ow.ly/QhutH
Or leave a review on the Amazon UK page: http://ow.ly/QhuF4

Online resources

Travel Information

- **Indie Traveller** – www.indietraveller.co (this is my blog!)
- **WikiVoyage** – www.wikivoyage.org (general travel/backpacker guide)
- **Wiki Overland** – www.wikioverland.org (for road tripping)
- **Travel Independent** – www.travelindependent.info
- **I Hate Taxis** – www.ihatetaxis.com (taxi fare information)
- **Sleeping In Airports** – www.sleepinginairports.net
- **TripAdvisor** – www.tripadvisor.com

Budgeting

- **Price of Travel** – www.priceoftravel.com
- **Budget Your Trip** – www.budgetyourtrip.com

Travel Communities

- **Lonely Planet Thorn Tree** – www.lonelyplanet.com/thorntree
- **Nomadic Matt's Forums** – http://forums.nomadicmatt.com/
- **Reddit** – www.reddit.com (check out /r/travel and /r/backpacking in particular)

Flight Booking

- **Momondo** – www.momondo.com
- **SkyScanner** – www.skyscanner.net
- **Kayak Explore** – www.kayak.com/explore

Hostel Bookings

- **Hostelworld** – www.hostelworld.com
- **Hostelbookers** – www.hostelbookers.com
- **Hostelrocket** – www.hostelrocket.com

Budget Hotel Bookings

- **Agoda** – www.agoda.com
- **Bookings.com** – www.bookings.com

Sharing Economy

- **Airbnb** – www.airbnb.com
- **CouchSurfing** – www.couchsurfing.org
- **Trampolinn** – www.trampolinn.com (CouchSurfing but with points)
- **TrustRoots** – www.trustroots.org (also similar to CouchSurfing)

Volunteering

- **WWOOF** – www.wwoof.net (volunteer placements on farms)
- **HelpX** – www.helpx.net

Local Guides

- **Vayable** – www.vayable.com
- **GetYourGuide** – www.getyourguide.com
- **WithLocals** – www.withlocals.com

Language Learning

- **Duolingo** – www.duolingo.com (free interactive language learning)
- **Memrise** – www.memrise.com (similar to Duolingo)
- **Fluent In 3 Months** – www.fluentin3months.com (blog on travel + language learning)

Visas

- **VisaHQ** – www.visahq.com

Acknowledgements

Much thanks to Duncan Fyfe, my editor for the 1st edition, who dared read and critique my embarrassing early drafts and who was of huge help in improving my writing.

A special thanks to my family for all their love, wisdom and encouragement.

Thanks to Yvonne for her excellent feedback based on her extensive experience travelling all over the world, including in some countries I have not yet been. Thanks also to Wout for his valuable input, and thanks to everyone else who read early versions of this book and gave their feedback or encouragement.

A big thanks to my friends at home, both in the UK and the Netherlands, who have had to put up with my constant travel ravings on Facebook for some time now. I miss you all when I am away.

Finally, a heartfelt thanks to the countless people I have met on my travels. Without you, my journeys would not have been meaningful. I hope to see you again someday, somewhere in the world.

23535437R00150

Printed in Poland
by Amazon Fulfillment
Poland Sp. z o.o., Wrocław